D0725378

Stuart Britain: A Very Short Introduction

VERY SHORT INTRODUCTIONS are for anyone wanting a stimulating and accessible way in to a new subject. They are written by experts, and have been published in more than 25 languages worldwide.

The series began in 1995, and now represents a wide variety of topics in history, philosophy, religion, science, and the humanities. Over the next few years it will grow to a library of around 200 volumes – a Very Short Introduction to everything from ancient Egypt and Indian philosophy to conceptual art and cosmology.

Very Short Introductions available now:

Available soon:

For more information visit our web site
www.oup.co.uk/vsi

John Morrill

STUART
BRITAIN

A Very Short Introduction

OXFORD

UNIVERSITY PRESS

Great Clarendon Street, Oxford OX2 6DP

Oxford University Press is a department of the University of Oxford.
It furthers the University's objective of excellence in research, scholarship,
and education by publishing worldwide in

Oxford New York

Auckland Bangkok Buenos Aires Cape Town Chennai
Dar es Salaam Delhi Hong Kong Istanbul Karachi Kolkata
Kuala Lumpur Madrid Melbourne Mexico City Mumbai Nairobi
São Paulo Shanghai Taipei Tokyo Toronto

Oxford is a registered trade mark of Oxford University Press
in the UK and in certain other countries

Published in the United States
by Oxford University Press Inc., New York

Text first published in *The Oxford Illustrated History of Britain* 1984
First published as a Very Short Introduction 2000

British Library Cataloguing in Publication Data

Data available

Library of Congress Cataloging in Publication Data

Data available

ISBN 0-19-285400-3

5 7 9 10 8 6

Typeset by RefineCatch Ltd, Bungay, Suffolk
Printed in Great Britain by
TJ International Ltd., Padstow, Cornwall

Dedication

For David Smith, my pupil in 1984 and my colleague in 2000, with gratitude for all his friendship and loyalty

Contents

List of Illustrations

List of Maps

Introduction

The Stuarts were one of England's least successful dynasties. Charles I was put on public trial for treason and was publicly beheaded; James II fled the country fearing a similar fate, and abandoned his kingdom and throne. James I and Charles II died peacefully in their beds, but James I lived to see all his hopes fade and ambitions thwarted, while Charles II, although he had the trappings of success, was a curiously unambitious man, whose desire for a quiet life was not achieved until it was too late for him to enjoy it. Towering above the Stuart age were the two decades of civil war, revolution, and republican experiment, which ought to have changed fundamentally the course of English history, but which did so, if at all, very elusively. Whilst kings and generals toiled and failed, however, a fundamental change was taking place in English economy and society, largely unheeded and certainly unfashioned by the will of government. In fact, the most obvious revolution in seventeenth-century England was the consequence of a decline in the birth-rate.

Chapter 1
Society and Economic Life

The population of England had been growing steadily from the early sixteenth century, if not earlier. It continued to grow in the first half of the seventeenth century. The total population of England in 1600 was probably fairly close to 4.1 million (and Scotland, Ireland, and Wales, much more impressionistically, 1.9 million). By the mid-century, the population of England had reached a peak of almost 5.3 million, and the total for Britain had risen from roughly 6.0 to roughly 7.7 million. Thereafter, the number stabilized, or may even have sagged to 4.9 million in England, 7.3 million in Britain. The reasons for the rise in population, basically a steady progression with occasional setbacks resulting from epidemics before 1650, and the subsequent relapse, are very puzzling. The best recent research has placed most emphasis on the family-planning habits of the population. Once the plague had lost its virulence, a country like England, in which land was plentiful and extremes of weather never such as to wipe out entire harvests, was likely to see population growth. Each marriage was likely to produce more than enough children who would survive to adulthood to maintain the population. The rate of population growth was in fact kept rather low by the English custom of late marriage. In all social groups, marriage was usually deferred until both partners were in their mid-twenties and the wife had only 12 to 15 childbearing years before her. The reason for this pattern of late marriage seems to be the firm convention that the couple save up enough money to launch themselves as an independent household before they wed. For the better off, this frequently meant delay until after several years at university, in legal training, or an apprenticeship of seven years or more; for the less well off a long term of domestic service, living in with all found but little in the way of cash wages.

This pattern continued into the late seventeenth century with even later marriage, perhaps because the real earnings of the young had fallen so that sufficient savings took longer to generate. At any rate the average age of first marriage for women seems to have risen by a further two years to over 26, with a consequent effect on fertility. More dramatic still is the evidence of a will to restrict family size. Steps were clearly taken in families with three or more children to prevent or inhibit further conceptions. For example, mothers would breast-feed third or subsequent children for many more months than they would their first or second child, with the (effective) intention of lowering fertility. Crude contraceptive devices and sexual prudence were also clearly widespread. Some studies of gentry families even suggest that celibacy became much more common (the massive growth of the navy may be partly responsible for this unexpected development!). In South Wales, one in three of all heads of leading gentry families remained unmarried in the late seventeenth century compared with a negligible proportion one hundred years earlier; while the average numbers of children per marriage declined from five to two and a half (which, given the high rate of child mortality, meant that a high proportion of those families died out). It is not known whether this was typical of the gentry everywhere or of other social groups. But it does graphically illustrate changing demographic patterns.

Consequences of Population Growth

The economic, social, and political consequences were momentous. In the century before 1640, population was growing faster than food resources. One result of this was occasional and localized food shortages so severe as to occasion hunger, starvation, and death. It is possible that some Londoners died of starvation at the end of the sixteenth and at the beginning of the seventeenth centuries and quite certain that many did so in Cumbria in the early 1620s. Thereafter, famine disappears as a visible threat, in England at least. Increased agricultural production, better communication and lines of credit, and the levelling off of population solved the problem. England escaped the periodic dearths and widespread starvation that were to continue to devastate its Continental neighbours for decades to come.

A more persistent effect of population growth was price inflation. Food prices rose eightfold in the period 1500–1640, wages less than threefold. For most of those who did not produce their own food, and enough of it to feed themselves and their household with a surplus to sell in the market, it was a century of financial attrition. Above all, for the growing proportion of the nation who depended upon wage-labouring, the century witnessed a major decline in living standards. In fact, a large section of the population – certainly a majority – had to buy much of their food, and these purchases took up an increasing proportion of their income. It became a central concern of government to regulate the grain trade and to provide both local machinery and an administrative code, backed up by legal sanctions, to ensure that whenever there was harvest failure, available stocks of grain and other produce were made widely available at the lowest extra cost which could be achieved.

A growing population put pressure not only on food resources but on land. With families producing on average more than one son, either family property had to be divided, reducing the endowment of each member for the next generation, or one son took over the family land or tenancy while the others had to fend for themselves. The high prices of agricultural produce made it worth while to plough, or otherwise to farm, marginal lands hitherto uneconomic, but in most regions by the early seventeenth century there was little unoccupied land left to be so utilized. The way forward lay with the more productive use of existing farmed land, particularly in woodland areas or in the Fenland where existing conditions (inundations by the sea or winter rain) made for only limited usage. The problem here was that the drainage of the Fens or the clearing of woodland areas was costly, had to be undertaken by those with risk capital, and had to be at the expense of the lifestyle, livelihood, and modest prosperity of those who lived there. Once again, government was forced to be active in mediating (or more often vacillating) between encouraging higher productivity and guarding against the anguish and protest of those adversely affected.

A growing population also put pressure on jobs. By the early seventeenth century there was widespread under-employment in England. Agriculture remained the major source of employment, but the work in the fields was seasonal and hundreds of thousands found lay labouring sufficient for part but not all of the year. Because, however, labour was plentiful and cheap, because most manufacturing relied exclusively on muscle power rather than a form of energy that would draw workers to its source, because raw materials walked about on, grew up out of, or lay dormant within the land, 'industry' in the seventeenth century took place in cottages and outbuildings of rural village communities. For some, especially in the metalworking and building trades, 'manufacturing' would be the primary source of income. For others, as in some textile trades, it could be a primary or secondary source of income. Textiles were by far the largest 'manufacture', with perhaps 200,000 workers scattered throughout England, above all in the south-west, in East Anglia, or in the Pennine region. It was a particularly volatile industry, however, with high food prices dampening the domestic market, and war and foreign competition sharply reducing foreign markets in the early seventeenth century. Tens of thousands of families, however, could not balance the household budget whatever they tried. Injury, disability, or death made them particularly vulnerable to a shortfall of revenue. There was chronic 'under-employment': a structural problem of too many part-time workers seeking full-time work.

To take just one example, at Aldenham in Hertfordshire, about one in ten households needed regular support from the poor rate but a further one in four (making over one-third in all) needed occasional doles or allowances (for example of fuel or clothes) to ease them through difficult patches. For a large number of families, achieving subsistence involved scrounging or scavenging fuel or wild fruit and vegetables and seeking periodic help from local charities or the rates – what has been called the 'economy of makeshifts'. One effect of the difficulties of rural employment was to drive large numbers of men and women into the cities – above all to London – where the problems were no fewer but rather more volatile. There was a large amount of casual unskilled labour in the towns, but casual work could shrink rapidly in times of recession or harvest failure. High food prices meant less demand for other goods and this in turn meant less scope for non-agricultural wages. Those who most needed additional wages for food were most likely to find less work available. Once more, the government had been drawn in to organize and superintend a national scheme of poor relief, and ancillary codes of practice governing geographical mobility, house building, and the promotion of overseas trade. Thus a growing population greatly increased the duties and responsibilities of the government – arguably beyond the Crown's resources and capacity. Those who produced and sold goods, those who could benefit from the land hunger in increased rents and dues, and those who serviced an increasingly complex and uncertain market in lands and goods (notably the lawyers) wanted to enjoy the fruits of their success; others looked to the Crown to prevent or to mitigate the effects of structural change. A dynamic economy is one in which government has to arbitrate between competing and irreconcilable interests. No wonder the Crown found itself disparaged and increasingly distrusted.

Agricultural Changes

By contrast, the late seventeenth century saw the easing, if not the disappearance, of these problems. The slight population decline in itself prevented the problems from getting worse. The upsurge in agricultural productivity was more important. The nature and extent of agricultural change in the seventeenth century is still much disputed. What is clear is that England ceased from about the 1670s to be a net importer of grain and became an exporter; indeed, bounties had to be introduced to ensure that surplus stocks were not hoarded. This remarkable turn-around may have been the result of a massive extension of the acreage under the plough – either by the ploughing of land not hitherto farmed or by land amelioration schemes. But it might also be the result of the introduction of new methods of farming which dramatically increased the yield per acre. By skilful alternation of crops and more extensive use of manure and fertilizers, it is possible to increase yields of grain and to sustain much greater livestock levels. Almost all the ideas which were to transform English agriculture down to the early nineteenth century were known about by 1660; indeed most of them had been tried and tested in the Netherlands. The problem is to discover how rapidly they were taken up. There was stubborn conservatism, especially among the yeomen; the good ideas lay mingled in the textbooks with some equally plausible ones which were in fact specious; the most effective methods required considerable rationalization of land use and some of them required high capital outlay. In the early part of the century, it seems likely that the most widespread innovations were not those which increased yields, but those which soaked up cheap surplus employment – especially 'industrial' cash crops that had to be turned into manufactures: dye crops, tobacco, mulberry trees (for silkworms). It was only when a falling population raised real wages and lowered grain prices that the impetus to increase productivity replaced the desire to extend the scale of operation as a primary motivation of the farmer. Changes in the way land was rented out also gave the landlord better prospects of seeing a return on the money he invested in land leased

d. 423.

THE
Engliſh Farrier,
OR,
Country-mans Treaſure.

Shewing approved Remedies to cure all
Diſeaſes, hurts, maymes, maladies and griefes, in Horſes:
and how to know the ſeverall Diſeaſes that breed in them,
with a deſcription of every Veine, how and when
to let them blood, according to the nature of
their Diſeaſes.

With directions to know the ſeverall Ages of them.

Faithfully ſet forth according to Art and approved experiment, for the benefit of Gentlemen, Farmers, Inholders, Huſ-
bandmen, and generally for all.

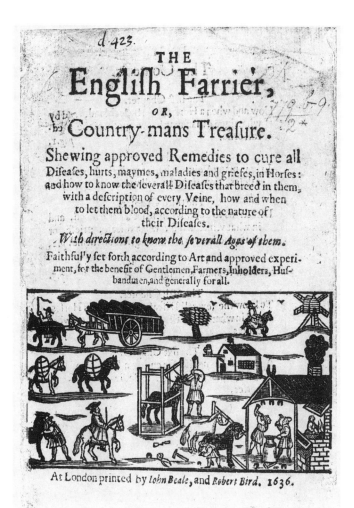

At London printed by *Iohn Beale*, and *Robert Bird*. 1636.

1. The title-page of one of the growing number of self-confident
agricultural tracts

F. H. Van Houe Sculp.

2. John Worlidge's design for a seed drill was one of the many new mechanical aids promoted during the century. It was also one of the many not to work

out. The new farming probably consolidated the position established earlier by the simple device of increasing the acreage under the plough. Either way, government action in the grain market and the regulation of wages became far less frequent and necessary.

Trade and Manufacturing

In 1600, England still consisted of a series of regional economies striving after, if not always achieving, self-sufficiency. Problems of credit and of distribution hindered the easy exchange of produce between regions. Most market towns, even the large county towns, were principally places where the produce of the area was displayed and sold. By 1690 this was no longer the case. England had for long been the largest free trade area in Europe, and had the Crown had its way at most points in the century, the full integration of Ireland and Scotland into a customs-free zone would have been achieved or brought nearer. That it was not so owed most to the narrow self-interest of lobbyists in the House of Commons, especially in the 1600s and the 1660s. No point in England was (or is) more than 75 miles from the sea, and as a result of the schemes to improve river navigation, few places by 1690 were more than 20 miles from waterways navigable to the sea. Gradually, a single, integrated national economy was emerging. No longer did each region have to strive for self-sufficiency, producing low-quality goods in poor-grade soil or inhospitable climate. Regional specializations could emerge, taking full advantage of soil and climatic conditions – specializations which could then be exchanged for surplus grain or dairy products from elsewhere. Hence, the spread of market-gardening in Kent.

Exactly the same could be said for manufactures. One consequence of and further stimulus to this was a retailing revolution – the coming of age of the shop. The characteristic of market towns was the market-stall or shambles, in which the stall-holders or retailers displayed their own wares which they had grown, made, or at least finished from local raw materials. By 1690, most towns, even quite small ones, had shops in the modern sense: places which did not distribute the produce of the region but which met the variegated needs of the region. The shopkeeper met those needs from far and wide. One particularly well-documented example is William Stout, who, in the 1650s, rented a shop in Lancaster for £5 per annum. He visited London and Sheffield and bought goods worth over £200, paid for half in cash (a legacy from his father), half on credit. Soon he was purchasing goods from far and wide and offering the people of Lancaster and its environs a wide variety of produce: West Indian sugar, American tobacco, West Riding ironmongery, and so on. Nonetheless, once towns became centres for the distribution of the produce of the world, people would tend to bypass the smaller towns with little choice and make for the bigger centres with maximum choice. This is why most seventeenth-century urban growth was concentrated in existing large market towns. The proportion of the population living in the twenty or so towns which already had 10,000 inhabitants rose sharply; the proportion living in the smaller market towns actually fell slightly. Some small centres of manufacturing (metalworking towns such as Birmingham and Sheffield, or cloth-finishing towns such as Manchester or Leeds, or shipbuilding towns such as Chatham) became notable urban centres. But the 20 largest towns in 1690 were almost the same as the 20 largest in 1600. All of them were on the coast or on navigable rivers.

Large Towns

Large towns, then, prospered because of their changing role in marketing. But many of them – and county towns especially – increasingly concentrated not only on the sale of goods; they began to concentrate on the sale of services. The pull of the shops and the burgeoning importance of county towns as local administrative centres, in which hundreds gathered regularly for local courts and commissions, encouraged the service and leisure industries. Gentlemen and prosperous farmers came to town for business or for the shops, and would stop to take professional advice from lawyers, doctors, estate agents; or bring their families and stay over for a round of social exchanges linked by visits to the theatre, concerts, or new recreational facilities. The age of the spa and the resort was dawning.

Paris, the largest town in France, had 350,000 inhabitants in the mid-seventeenth century. The second and third largest were Rouen and Lyons with 80,000–100,000 inhabitants. In Europe, there were only five towns with populations of more than 250,000, but over one hundred with more than 50,000 inhabitants. In England, however, London had well over half a million inhabitants by 1640 or 1660; Newcastle, Bristol, and Norwich, which rivalled one another for second place, had barely 25,000 each. London was bigger than the next 50 towns in England combined. It is hard to escape the conclusion that London was growing at the expense of the rest. Its stranglehold on overseas trade, and therefore on most of the early banking and financial activity, was slow to ease; in consequence much of the trade from most of the outports had to be directed via London. In the seventeenth century the major new 're-export' trades (the importation of colonial raw materials such as sugar and tobacco for finishing and dispatch to Europe) were concentrated there. London dominated the governmental, legal, and political world. While rural England flourished under the opportunities to feed the capital and keep its inhabitants warm, urban growth was probably slowed. By 1640, 10 per cent of the population lived in the capital, and one in six had lived part of their lives there. By 1690 the richest 100 Londoners were among the richest men in England. No longer was wealth primarily the perquisite of the landed.

Migration

If goods moved more freely within a national economy, people may have become more rooted in their own community. Both before and after the Civil War, more than two-thirds of all English people died in a parish different from the one in which they were born. But both before and after the wars, most did not move far; most stayed within their county of birth. It is possible to distinguish two patterns of migration. The first is 'betterment migration', as adolescents and young adults moved to take up apprenticeship or tenancies of farms. This migration throughout the century was essentially local except for movement from all over the country to London for apprenticeships. The second is 'subsistence migration', as those who found no work or prospect of work at home took to the road, often travelling long distances in the hope of finding employment elsewhere. Such migration was far more common in the first half of the century than in the second, partly because demographic stagnation and economic development created a better chance of jobs at home, partly because the general easing of demands on poor relief made parish authorities more sympathetic to the able-bodied unemployed, and partly because tough settlement laws inhibited and discouraged migration. An Act of Parliament in 1662 gave constables and overseers power to punish those who moved from parish to parish in search of vacant common land or wasteland on which to build cottages.

The seventeenth century is probably the first in English history in which more people emigrated than immigrated. In the course of the century, something over one-third of a million people – mainly young adult males – emigrated across the Atlantic. The largest single group made for the West Indies; a second substantial group made for Virginia and for Catholic Maryland; a very much smaller group made for Puritan New England. The pattern of emigration was a fluctuating one, but it probably reached its peak in the 1650s and 1660s. For most of those who went, the search for employment and a better life was almost certainly the principal cause of their departure. For a clear minority, however, freedom from religious persecution and the expectation that they could establish churches to worship God in their preferred fashion took precedence. An increasing number were forcibly transported as a punishment for criminal acts or (particularly in the 1650s) simply as a punishment for vagrancy. In addition to the transatlantic settlers, an unknown number crossed the English Channel and settled in Europe. The largest group were probably the sons of Catholic families making for religious houses or mercenary military activity. Younger sons of Protestant gentlemen also enlisted in the latter. Many hundreds were to return to fight the English Civil War. Thus, whereas the sixteenth century had seen England become a noted haven for religious refugees, in the seventeenth century Europe and America received religious refugees from England. There was probably less immigration in the first and second quarters of the seventeenth century than in any quarter of the previous century. The only significant immigration in the seventeenth century was of Jews, who flocked in after the Cromwellian regime had removed the legal bars on their residence, and of French Huguenots escaping from Louis XIV's persecution in the 1650s.

Fewer men set up home far from the place of their birth. But many more men travelled the length and breadth of England. There was a tripling or a quadrupling of the number of packmen, carriers, and others engaged in moving goods about. The tunnage of shipping engaged in coastal trading probably rose by the same amount. The roads were thronged with petty chapmen, with their news-sheets, tracts, almanacs, cautionary tales, pamphlets full of homespun wisdom; pedlars with trinkets of all sorts; and travelling entertainers. If the alehouse had always been a distraction from that other social centre of village life, the parish church, it now became much more its rival in the dissemination of news and information and in the formation of popular culture. In the early years of the century, national and local regulation of alehouses was primarily concerned with ensuring that not too much of the barley harvest was malted and brewed; by the end of the century, regulation was more concerned with the pub's potential for sedition.

Redistribution of Wealth

In the century from 1540 to 1640 there was a redistribution of wealth away from rich and poor towards those in the middle of society. The richest men in the kingdom derived the bulk of their income from rents and services, and these were notoriously difficult to keep in line with inflation: a tradition of long leases and the custom of fixed rents and fluctuating 'entry fines' – payments made when tenancies changed hands – militated against it. Vigilant landowners could keep pace with inflation, but many were not vigilant. Equally, those whose farms or holdings did not make them self-sufficient suffered from rising (and worse, fluctuating) food prices, while a surplus on the labour market and declining real wages made it very hard for the poor to make good the shortfall. The number of landless labourers and cottagers soared. Those in the middle of society, whether yeomen farmers or tradesmen, prospered. If they produced a surplus over and above their own needs, they could sell dear and produce more with the help of cheap labour. They could lend their profits to their poorer neighbours (there were after all no banks, stocks and shares, building societies) and foreclose on the debts. They invested in more land, preferring to extend the scale of their operations rather than sink capital into improved productivity. Many of those who prospered from farming rose into the gentry. Only two groups had 'social' status in seventeenth-century England – the gentry and the peerage. Everybody else had 'economic' status, and was defined by economic function (husbandman, cobbler, merchant, attorney, etc.). The peerage and gentry were different. They had a 'quality' which set them apart. That 'quality' was 'nobility'. Peers and the gentry were 'noble'; everybody else was 'ignoble' or 'churlish'. Such concepts were derived partly from the feudal and chivalric traditions in which land was held from the Crown in exchange for the performance of military duties. These duties had long since disappeared, but the notion that the ownership of land and 'manors' conferred status and 'honour' had been reinvigorated by the appropriation to English conditions of Aristotle's notion of the citizen. The gentleman or nobleman was a man set apart to govern. He was independent and leisured: he derived his income without having to work for it, that income made him free from want and from being beholden to or dependent upon others, and he had the time and leisure to devote himself to the arts of government.

He was independent in judgement and trained to make decisions. Not all gentlemen served in the offices which required such qualities (justice of the peace, sheriff, militia captain, high constable, etc.). But all had this capacity to serve, to govern. A gentleman was expected to be hospitable, charitable, fair-minded. He was distinguished from his country neighbour, the yeoman, as much by attitude of mind and personal preference as by wealth. Minor gentry and yeomen had similar incomes. But they lived different lives: the gentleman rented out his lands, wore cloth and linen, read Latin; the yeoman was a working farmer, wore leather, read and wrote in English. By 1640, there were perhaps 120 peers and 20,000 gentry, 1 in 20 of all adult males. The permanence of land and the security of landed income restricted gentility to the countryside; the prosperous merchant or craftsman, though he may have had a larger income than many gentlemen, and have discharged, in the government of his borough, the same duties, was denied the status of gentleman. He had to work, and his capital and income were insecure. Younger sons of gentlemen, trained up in the law or apprenticed into trade, did not retain their status. But they were put into professions through which they or their sons could redeem it. The wealthy merchant or lawyer had some prospect of buying a manor and settling back into a gentler lifestyle at the end of his life.

This pattern shifted in the late seventeenth century. Conditions were now against the larger farmer: he had high taxation, higher labour costs, and lower profits, unless he invested heavily in higher productivity, which he was less able to do than the great landowners (for whom there were economies of scale). Few yeomen now aspired to the trappings of gentility, while many minor gentlemen abandoned an unequal struggle to keep up appearances. On the other hand, professional men, merchants, and town governors became bolder in asserting that they were as good as the country gentleman and were entitled to his title of respect. The definition of 'gentility' was stretched to include them without a prior purchase of land. This 'pseudo-gentility' became increasingly respectable and increasingly widely recognized, even by the heralds. It was not, however, recognized by many country gentlemen, who bitterly resented this devaluation of their treasured status. They responded to the debasement of the term 'gentry' by sponsoring and promoting a new term which restored their exclusiveness and self-importance: they called themselves squires and their group the 'squirearchy'.

The century between 1540 and 1640 had seen the consolidation of those in the middle of society at the expense of those at the bottom and, to some extent, of those at the top. The century after 1640 saw some relief for the mass of poor householders, increasing difficulties for large farmers and small landowners, rich pickings for those at the top. There was emerging by 1690 (though its great age was just beginning) a group of men whose interests, wealth, and power grew out of, but extended far beyond, their landed estates. They invested in trade, in government loans, in the mineral resources of their land, as well as in improved farming and in renting out farming land. They spent as much time in their town houses as in their country seats; they were as much at home with the wealthy elite in London as with their rural neighbours. They constituted a culturally cosmopolitan elite of transcendent wealth, incorporating many of the peerage, but not confined to them. This new phenomenon was recognized at the time and needed a label, a collective noun. It became known as the aristocracy (a term hitherto a preserve of political thinkers, like democracy, rather than of social analysis). The invention of the term 'squire' and adaptation of the word 'aristocrat' in the late seventeenth century tells us a great deal about the way society was evolving. The integration of town and country, the spread of metropolitan values and fashions, the fluidity of the economy, and the mobility of society are all involved in the way people categorized one another. By 1690, England already had a flexible and simple moneyed elite; access to wealth and power was not restricted by outdated notions of privilege and obsessions with purity of birth as in much of Europe.

Chapter 2
Government and Law

Stuart governments had little understanding of these structural changes and less ability to influence them. The resources of Stuart government fell far short of those required to carry out the ambitions and expectations which most people had of their king and which kings had of themselves.

Financial Resources

The financial and bureaucratic resources at the disposal of rulers remained limited. James I inherited an income of £350,000 a year. By the later 1630s this had risen to £1,000,000 a year and by the 1650s to £2,000,000 a year. This is a notable increase. It meant that, throughout the seventeenth century, the Stuarts could finance their activities in peacetime. As the century wore on, revenues from Crown lands and Crown feudal and prerogative right fell away to be an insignificant part of royal revenues. The ordinary revenues of the Crown became predominantly those derived from taxing trade: customs duties on the movement of goods into and out of the country and excise duties, a sales tax on basic consumer goods (above all beer). Only during the Civil Wars and interregnum (when a majority of State revenues came from property taxes) did direct taxation play a major part in the budget. Over the period 1603–40 and 1660–89, less than 8 per cent of all royal revenues came from direct taxation – certainly less than in the fourteenth or sixteenth centuries. This, in part, reflects landowner domination of the tax-granting House of Commons; but it also reflects an administrative arthritis that hindered improvements in the efficiency and equity of tax distribution.

The buoyancy of trade, especially after 1630, was the greatest single cause of the steady growth in royal income – well ahead of inflation – that made Stuart monarchy at almost every point the least indebted in Europe. Both James I and Charles II suffered from fiscal incontinence, buying the loyalty and favour of their servants with a rashness that often went beyond what was necessary. However, the problems of the Stuarts can fairly be laid at Elizabeth's door. All over Europe in the sixteenth and seventeenth centuries, princes used the threat of invasion by tyrannical and/or heretical foreigners to create new forms of taxation, which were usually made permanent when the invasion scare had receded or was repulsed. William III was to make just such a transformation in the 1690s when England was under siege from the absolutist Louis XIV and the bigoted James II. Since the Stuarts never faced a realistic threat of invasion, they never had a good excuse to insist on unpalatable fiscal innovations. Elizabeth I had a perfect opportunity in the Armada years but she was too old, too conservatively advised, and too preoccupied even to attempt it. Instead she paid for the war by selling land. Although this did not make James I's and Charles I's position as difficult as was once thought, it did have one major consequence: it deprived the king of security against loans.

The Stuarts, then, whenever they put their mind to it, had an adequate income and a balanced budget. Almost alone amongst the rulers of the day they never went bankrupt, and only once, in 1670, had to defer payment of interest on loans. But they never had enough money to wage successful war. Since, throughout the century up to 1689, no one ever threatened to invade or declare war on England , this was not as serious as it sounds. England waged war on Spain (1624–30, 1655–60), on France (1627–30), and on the Netherlands (1651–4, 1665–7, 1672–4), but always as the aggressor. It cannot be said that these wars achieved the objectives of those who advocated them, but none was lost in the sense that concessions were made on the status quo ante. While rivalries in the colonial spheres (South Asia, Africa, and North, Central, and South America) were intensifying, no territories were ceded and expansion continued steadily. There was a growing recognition of the futility of major armed interventions on the Continent, which led to gradual increases in the proportion of resources devoted to the navy, while all Continental countries found that the costs of land warfare hindered the development of their navies. By 1689 the British navy was the equal of the Dutch and the French, and the wars of the next 25 years were to make it the dominant navy in Europe. For a country which could not afford an active foreign policy, England's standing in the world had improved remarkably during the century.

The Army

The monarchy lacked coercive power: there was no standing army or organized police force. Even the guards regiments which protected the king and performed ceremonial functions around him were a Restoration creation. In the period 1603–40 the number of fighting men upon whom the king could call in an emergency could be counted in scores rather than in thousands. After 1660 there were probably about 3,000 armed men on permanent duty in England and rather more in Ireland and Tangiers (which had come to Charles II as a rather troublesome part of the dowry of his Portuguese wife). There were then also several thousand Englishmen regimented and in permanent service with the Dutch and with the Portuguese armies who could be recalled in emergency. But there was no military presence in England, and apart from pulling up illegal tobacco crops in the West Country and occasionally rounding up religious dissidents, the army was not visible until James II's reign.

It had not been so, of course, in the aftermath of the Civil War. At the height of the conflict, in 1643–4, there were probably 150,000 men in arms: one in eight of the adult male population. By the late 1640s, this had fallen to 25,000. The number rose to 45,000 in the wars waged against the youthful Charles II and the Scots (1650–1), and then fell to remain at between 10,000 and 14,000 for the rest of the decade (although between 15,000 and 40,000 more were serving at any particular moment in Scotland and Ireland). The troops in England were widely dispersed into garrisons. London had a very visible military presence, since 3,000 or so troops were kept in very public places (including St Paul's Cathedral, the nave of which became a barracks). Everywhere troops could be found meddling in local administration and local politics (and perhaps above all in local churches, for garrisons very often protected and nurtured radical, separatist meeting-houses). The army was at once the sole guarantor of minority republican governments, and a source of grievance which hindered long-term acceptance of the regicide and revolution by the population at large.

Throughout the rest of the century, then, the first line of defence against invasion and insurrection was not a standing army but the militia: half-trained, modestly equipped, often chaotically organized local defence forces mustered and led by local gentry families appointed by the Crown but not subservient to it. They saw active service or fired shots in anger only as part of the war effort in 1642–5.

There was no police force at all. Few crimes were 'investigated' by the authorities. Criminal trials resulted from accusations and evidence brought by victims or aggrieved parties to the attention of the justices of the peace. Arrests were made by village constables (ordinary farmers or craftsmen taking their turn for a year) or by sheriffs (gentlemen also taking their turn) who did have a small paid staff of bailiffs. Riots and more widespread disorders could only be dealt with by the militia or by a 'posse comitatus', a gathering of freeholders specially recruited for the occasion by the sheriff.

3. Execution of the Gunpowder Plotters. The penalty exacted for treason – hanging, disembowelling, and quartering – is powerfully represented

Bureaucratic Resources

The Crown had little coercive power; it also had little bureaucratic muscle. The total number of paid public officials in the 1630s was under 2,000, half of them effectively private domestic servants of the king (cooks, stable boys, etc.). The 'civil service' which governed England, or at any rate was paid to govern England, numbered less than 1,000. Most remarkable was the smallness of the clerical staff servicing the courts of law and the Privy Council. The volume of information at the fingertips of decision-makers was clearly restricted by the lack of fact-gatherers and the lack of filing cabinets for early retrieval of the information which was available. In the course of the seventeenth century there was a modest expansion of the civil service with significant improvements in naval administration and in the finance departments (with the emergence of the Treasury as a body capable of establishing departmental budgets and fiscal priorities). Two invaluable by-products of the Civil War itself were the introduction of arabic numerals instead of Roman ones in official accounts and of the printed questionnaire. Although the Privy Council trebled in size in the period 1603–40 and doubled again under Charles II, there was a steady decrease in efficiency, and the introduction of subcommittees of the Council for foreign affairs, trade, the colonies, etc. did not improve on Elizabethan levels of efficiency.

Government in seventeenth-century England was by consent. By this we usually mean government by and through Parliament. But, more important, it meant government by and through unpaid, voluntary officials throughout England. County government was in the hands of 3,000 or so prominent gentry in the early seventeenth century, 5,000 or so in the late seventeenth century. They were chosen by the Crown, but that freedom of choice was effectively limited in each county to a choice of 50 or so of the top 80 families by wealth and reputation. In practice all but heads of gentry families who were too young, too old, too mad, or too Catholic were appointed. In the 200 or so corporate boroughs, power lay with corporations of 12–100 men. In most boroughs these men constituted a self-perpetuating oligarchy; in a large minority, election was on a wider franchise. Only in the 1680s was any serious attempt made to challenge the prescriptive rights of rural and urban elites to exercise power.

Local Elites

The significance of the government's dependence on the voluntary support of local elites cannot be overestimated. They controlled the assessment and collection of taxation; the maintenance, training, and deployment of the militia; the implementation of social and economic legislation; the trial of most criminals; and, increasingly, the enforcement of religious uniformity. Their autonomy and authority was actually greater in the Restoration period than in the pre-war period (the Restoration settlement was a triumph for the country gentry rather than for king or Parliament). The art of governing in the seventeenth century was the art of persuading those who ruled in town and country that there was a close coincidence of interest between themselves and the Crown. For most of the time, this coincidence of interest was recognized. Crown and gentry shared a common political vocabulary; they shared the same conception of society; they shared the same anxieties about the fragility of order and stability. This constrained them to obey the Crown even when it went against the grain. As one gentleman put it to a friend who complained about having to collect possibly illegal taxes in 1625: 'we must not give an example of disobedience to those beneath us'. Local elites were also engaged in endless local disputes, rivalries, and conflicts of interest. These might involve questions of procedure or honour; the distribution of taxation or rates; or promotion to local offices; or the desirability of laying out money to improve highways or rivers. In all these cases the Crown and the Privy Council were the obvious arbitrator. All local governors needed royal support to sustain their local influence. None could expect to receive that support if he did not co-operate with the Crown most of the time. The art of government was to keep all local governors on a treadmill of endeavour. In the period 1603–40 most governors did their duty even when they were alarmed or dismayed at what was asked of them; after 1660 the terrible memories of the Civil War had the same effect. Only when Charles I in 1641 and James II in 1687 calculatingly abandoned the bargain with those groups with the bulk of the land, wealth, and power did that coincidence of interest dissolve.

In maintaining that coincidence of outlook we should not underestimate the strength of royal control of those institutions which moulded belief and opinion. The Crown's control of schools and universities, of pulpits, of the press was never complete, and it may have declined with time. But most teachers, preachers, and writers, most of the time, upheld royal authority and sustained established social and religious views. This is perhaps most clearly seen in the speed with which the ideas of Archbishop Laud and his clique (which, as we shall see, sought to revolutionize the Church of England) were disseminated at Oxford and Cambridge, through carefully planted dons, to a whole generation of undergraduates. Equally the strength of divine-right theories of monarchy was far greater in the 1680s amongst the graduate clergy than in the population at large, again as a result of the Crown's control over key appointments in the universities. At the Restoration, the earl of Clarendon told Parliament that Cromwell's failure to regulate schoolmasters and tutors was a principal reason why Anglicanism had thrived in the 1650s and emerged fully clad with the return of the king: he pledged the government to ensure the political loyalty and religious orthodoxy of all who set up as teachers, and there is evidence that this was more effectively done in the late seventeenth century than at any other time. Even after 1689, when the rights of religious assembly were conceded to Dissenters, they were denied the right to open or run their own schools or academies.

Chapter 3
The Early Stuarts

The Crown, therefore, had formidable, but perishable, assets. There was nothing inexorable either about the way the Tudor political system collapsed, causing civil war and revolution, or about the way monarchy and Church returned and re-established themselves. Fewer men feared or anticipated, let alone sought, civil war in the 1620s or 1630s than had done so in the 1550s and 1590s. Few people felt any confidence in the 1660s and 1670s that republicanism and religious fanaticism had been dealt an irrevocable blow.

Moving away from Civil War

Throughout Elizabeth's reign, there was a triple threat of civil war: over the wholly uncertain succession; over the passions of rival religious parties; and over the potential interest of the Continental powers in English and Irish domestic disputes. All these extreme hazards had disappeared or receded by the 1620s and 1630s. The Stuarts were securely on the throne with undisputed heirs; the English Catholic community had settled for a deprived status but minimal persecution (they were subject to discriminatory taxes and charges and denied access to public office), while the Puritan attempt to take over the Church by developing their own organizations and structures within it had been defeated. A Puritan piety and zeal was widespread, but its principal characteristic was now to accept the essential forms and practices of the Prayer Book and the canons but to supplement and augment them by their own additional services, preachings, and prayer meetings. Above all, they sought to bring a spiritualization to the household that did not challenge but supplemented parochial worship. These additional forms were the kernel and the Prayer Book services the husk of their Christian witness, but the degree of confrontation between Puritans and the authorities decreased, and the ability of Puritans to organize an underground resistance movement to ungodly kings had vanished. Finally, the decline of internal tensions and the scale of conflicts on the Continent itself removed the incentive for other kings to interfere in England's domestic affairs. In all these ways, England was moving away from civil war in the early seventeenth century.

Furthermore, there is no evidence of a general decline into lawlessness and public violence: quite the reverse. Apart from a momentary spasm induced by the earl of Essex's attempts to overturn his loss of position at court, the period 1569–1642 is the longest period of domestic peace which England had ever enjoyed. No peer and probably no gentleman was tried for treason between 1605 and 1641. Indeed, only one peer was executed during that period (Lord Castlehavon in 1631, for almost every known sexual felony). The number of treason trials and executions in general declined decade by decade.

Early Stuart England was probably the least violent country in Europe. There were probably more dead bodies on stage during a production of *Hamlet* or *Titus Andronicus* than in any one violent clash or sequence of clashes over the first 40 years of the century. Blood feuds and cycles of killings by rival groups were unheard of. England had no brigands, bandits, or even groups of armed vagabonds, other than occasional gatherings of 'Moss Troopers' in the Scottish border regions. While the late sixteenth century could still see rivalries and disputes amongst county justices flare up into fisticuffs and drawn swords (as in Cheshire in the 1570s and Nottinghamshire in the 1590s), respect for the institutions of justice was sufficient to prevent a perpetuation of such violence into the seventeenth century.

Englishmen were notoriously litigious, but that represented a willingness to submit to the arbitration of the king's courts. There was still much rough justice, many packed juries, much intimidation, and many informal community sanctions against offenders. But it stopped short of killings. A random fanatic stabbed the duke of Buckingham to death in 1628, but few if any other officers of the Crown – lords-lieutenant, deputy lieutenants, justices of the peace, or sheriffs – were slaughtered or maimed in the execution of their duty. A few bailiffs distraining the goods of those who refused to pay rates or taxes were beaten up or chased with pitchforks, but generally speaking the impression of law and order in the early decades is one of the omnicompetence of royal justice and one of a spectacular momentum of obedience in the major endeavours of government. It even seems likely that riots (most usually concerned with grain shortages, or the enclosure of common land depriving cottagers and artisans of rights essential to the family economy) were declining in frequency and intensity decade by decade. Certainly the degree of violence was strictly limited and few if any persons were killed during riots. The response of the authorities was also restrained: four men were executed for involvement in a riot at Maldon in 1629 just weeks after the quelling of a previous riot. Otherwise, the authorities preferred to deploy minimum force and to impose suspended sentences and to offer arbitration along with or instead of prosecutions. Riots posed no threat to the institutions of the State or to the existing social order.

The fact that few contemporaries expected a civil war may only mean that major structural problems went unrecognized. England may have been becoming ungovernable. The fact that neither crew nor passengers of an aircraft anticipate a crash does not prevent that crash. But while planes sometimes crash because of metal fatigue or mechanical failure, they also sometimes crash because of pilot error. The causes of the English Civil War are too complex to be explained in terms of such a simple metaphor, but it does seem that the war was more the consequence of pilot error than of mechanical failure.

When, with the wisdom of hindsight, contemporaries looked back at the causes of the 'Great Rebellion', they very rarely went back before the accession of Charles I in 1625. They were probably right.

James I

James I was, in many ways, a highly successful king. This was despite some grave defects of character and judgement. He was the very reverse of Queen Elizabeth. He had a highly articulate, fully developed, and wholly consistent view of the nature of monarchy and of kingly power – and he wholly failed to live up to it. He was a major intellectual, writing theoretical works on government and engaging effectively in debate with leading Catholic polemicists on theological and political issues, as well as turning his mind and his pen to the ancient but still growing threat of witchcraft, and to the recent and menacing introduction of tobacco. He believed that kings derived their authority directly from God and were answerable to God alone for the discharge of that trust. But James also believed that he was in practice constrained by solemn oaths made at his coronation to rule according to the 'laws and customs of the realm'. However absolute kings might be in the abstract, in the actual situation in which he found himself, he accepted that he could only make law and raise taxation in Parliament, and that every one of his actions as king was subject to judicial review. His prerogative, derived though it was from God, was enforceable only under the law. James was, in this respect, as good as his word. He had several disagreements with his Parliaments, or at any rate with groups of members of Parliament, but these differences were mostly unnecessary and of temporary effect. Thus he lectured the Commons in 1621 that their privileges derived from his gift, and this led to a row about their origins. But he was only claiming a right to comment on their use of his gift; he was not claiming, and at no point in relation to any such rights and liberties did he claim, that he had the right to revoke such gifts. It was this tactlessness, this ability to make the right argument at the wrong moment, that earned him Henry IV of France's sobriquet, 'the wisest fool in Christendom'.

His greatest failings, however, were not intellectual but moral and personal. He was an undignified figure, unkempt, uncouth, unsystematic, and fussy. He presided over a court where peculation and the enjoyment of perquisites rapidly obstructed efficient and honest government. Royal poverty made some remuneration of officials from tainted sources unavoidable. But under James (though not under his son) this got out of hand.

The public image of the court was made worse by a series of scandals involving sexual offences and murder. At one point in 1619 a former lord chamberlain, a former lord treasurer, a former secretary of state, and a former captain of the Gentlemen Pensioners all languished in the Tower on charges of a sexual or financial nature. In 1618, the king's latent homosexuality gave way to a passionate affair with a young courtier of minor gentry background, who rose within a few years to become duke of Buckingham, the first non-royal duke to be created for over a century. Buckingham was to take over the reins of government from the ailing James and to hold them for the young and prim Charles I, until his assassination in 1628. Such a poor public image cost the king dear. His lack of fiscal self-restraint both heightened his financial problem and reduced the willingness of the community at large to grant him adequate supply.

James I was a visionary king, and in terms of his own hopes and ambitions he was a failure. His vision was one of unity. He hoped to extend the union of the Crowns of England and Scotland into a fuller union of the kingdoms of Britain. He wanted full union of laws, of parliaments, of churches; he had to settle for a limited economic union, a limited recognition of joint citizenship, and a common flag. The sought-after 'union of hearts and minds' completely eluded him. James's vision was expressed in flexible, gradualist proposals. It was wrecked by the small-mindedness and negative reflexes of the parliamentary county gentry. He also sought to use the power and authority of his three crowns – England, Scotland, and Ireland – to promote the peace and unity of Christian princes, an aim which produced solid achievements in James's arbitration in the Baltic and in Germany in his early years, but which was discredited in his later years by his inability to prevent the outbreak of the Thirty Years War and the renewed conflict in the Low Countries. Finally, he sought to use his position as head of the 'Catholic and Reformed' Church of England, and as the promoter of co-operation between the Presbyterian Scots and episcopal English Churches, to advance the reunion of Christian Churches. His attempts to arrange an ecumenical council and the response of moderates in all churches, Catholic, orthodox, Lutheran, and Calvinist, to his calls for an end to religious strife were again wrecked by the outbreak of the Thirty Years War. But they had struck a resonant chord in many quarters.

James's reign did see, however, the growth of political stability in England, a lessening of religious passions, domestic peace, and the continuing respect of the international community. His 'plantation policy' in Ulster, involving the dispossession of native Irish Catholic landowners and their replacement by thousands of families from England (many of them in and around Londonderry settled by a consortium of Londoners) and (even more) from south-west Scotland, can also be counted a rather heartless short-term success, though its consequences are – all too grimly – still with us. He left large debts, a court with an unsavoury reputation, and a commitment to fight a limited war with Spain without adequate financial means.

He had squabbled with his Parliament and had failed to secure some important measures which he had propounded to them: of these, the Act of Union with Scotland and an elaborate scheme, known as the Great Contract, for rationalizing his revenues were the only ones that mattered. But he had suffered no major defeat at their hands in the sense that Parliament failed to secure any reduction in royal power and had not enhanced its own participation in government by one jot. Parliament met when the king chose and was dismissed when its usefulness was at an end. Procedural developments were few and had no bearing on parliamentary power. Parliament had sat for less than one month in six during the reign and direct taxation counted for less than one-tenth of the total royal budget. Most members recognized that its very survival as an institution was in serious doubt. No one believed that the disappearance of Parliament gave them the right, let alone the opportunity, to resist the king. James was a Protestant king who ruled under law. He generated distaste in some, but distrust and hatred in few if any, of his subjects. Charles I's succession in 1625 was the most peaceful and secure since 1509, and arguably since 1307.

Charles I

Just as there is a startling contrast between Elizabeth I and James I so there is between James I and Charles I. Where James was an informal, scruffy, approachable man, Charles was glacial, prudish, withdrawn, and shifty. He was a runt, a weakling brought up in the shadow of an accomplished elder brother who died of smallpox when Charles was 12. Charles was short, a stammerer, a man of deep indecision who tried to simplify the world around him by persuading himself that where the king led by example and where order and uniformity were set forth, obedience and peace would follow. He was one of those politicians so confident of the purity of his own motives and actions, so full of rectitude, that he saw no need to explain his actions or justify his conduct to his people. He was an inaccessible king except to his confidants. He was a silent king where James was voluble, a king assertive by deed not word. He was in many ways the icon that James had described in *Basilikon Doron*.

Government was very differently run. Charles was a chaste king who presided over a chaste court; venality and peculation were stanched; in

4. Charles I on horseback. Sir Anthony Van Dyck invokes the king as emperor and as Knight of St George, a potent symbol of authority and of a discipline that brought order and tranquillity. Charles surveys a gentle, tamed landscape

the years of peace after 1629 the budgets were balanced, the administration streamlined, and the Privy Council reorganized. In many respects, government was made more efficient and effective. But a heavy price was paid. In part this was due to misunderstandings and to failures of communication. The years 1625–30 saw England at war with Spain (to regain the territories seized from Charles's brother-in-law the elector Palatine and generally to support the Protestant cause) and with France (to make Louis XIII honour the terms of the marriage treaty uniting his sister Henrietta Maria to Charles I). Parliament brayed for war but failed to provide the supply to make the campaigns a success. A mercenary army was sent in vain into Germany; naval expeditions were mounted against French and Spanish coastal strongholds. Nothing was achieved. The administrative and military preparations themselves, together with financial devices resorted to in order to make good the deficiencies of parliamentary supply, were seen as oppressive and burdensome by many and as of dubious legality by some.

Throughout his reign, however, Charles blithely ruled as he thought right and did little to explain himself. By 1629, king and Parliament had had a series of confrontations over the failure of his foreign policy, over the fiscal expedients needed to finance that policy, over the use of imprisonment to enforce those expedients, and over the king's sponsorship of a new minority group within the Church whose beliefs and practices sharply diverged from the developing practice and teachings of the Anglican mainstream. In 1629, passions and frustrations reached such a peak that Charles decided that for the foreseeable future he would govern without calling Parliament. He probably believed that if the generation of hotheads and malcontents who had dominated recent sessions was allowed to die off, then the old harmony between king and Parliament could be restored. It was as simplistic as most of his assessments. But the decision was not in itself self-destructive. The three Parliaments of 1625–9 had been bitter and vindictive. But they represented a range of frustrations rather than an organized resistance. They also demonstrated the institutional impotence of Parliament. There was much outspoken criticism of royal policies, but no unity of criticism. Some MPs were anxious about the Crown's religious and foreign policies, others with the legal basis of the fiscal expedients. There was little that men such as John Pym, Sir Edward Coke, Sir Thomas Wentworth, Sir John Eliot, and Dudley Digges (to name perhaps the most vociferous royal critics in those sessions) shared beyond a detestation of Buckingham and the belief that the misgovernment of the present was best put right by their own entry into office. All were aspirant courtiers both because of the rewards and honours that would flow from office, and because of the principles and policies they would be able to advance. No change of political institutions and no change in the constitution was envisaged. They were not proto-revolutionaries; they lacked the unity of purpose even to stand forth as an alternative government team.

So in the 1630s the king ruled without Parliament and in the absence of any concerted action, peaceful or otherwise, to bring back Parliament. The king raised substantial revenues, adequate for peacetime purposes, and he faced obstruction, and that largely ineffective obstruction, in only one instance – the Ship Money rates used to build a fleet from 1634 onwards. Most of this obstruction was based on local disputes about the distribution of the rate, and over 90 per cent of it was collected, if rather more slowly than anticipated. Arguments about the legality of the measure were heard in open court and after the king's victory payments were resumed at a high level. By 1637 Charles was at the height of his power. He had a balanced budget, effective social and economic policies, an efficient council, and a secure title. There was a greater degree of political acquiescence than there had been for centuries.

Religious Policies

Charles was, however, alienating a huge majority of his people by his religious policies, for his support for Archbishop William Laud was re-creating some of the religious passions of the 1570s and 1580s. But it

5. William Laud, archbishop of Canterbury. All other sitters for Van Dyck are presented against a background that expresses their political, religious, and cultural values. Laud is presented as a simple cleric with no other pretensions

was not leading to the development of an underground Church or of subversive religious activity. Indeed, those who found the religious demands of Laud unacceptable now had an option not available to previous generations: they could and did emigrate to the New World. There, freed from the persecution of the Anglican authorities, they set about persecuting one another in the name of Protestant purity.

There were, however, two things about Laud which dangerously weakened loyalty to the Crown. One was that the teachings of many of those sponsored by the archbishop, and many of the practices encouraged by Laud himself and his colleagues, were reminiscent of Roman Catholic beliefs and ritual. With Laud himself maintaining that the Roman Church was a true Church, though a corrupt one, it became widely believed that popery was being let in by a side door, that the Anglican Church was being betrayed and abandoned. Laud's own priorities were not, in fact, intended to change the liturgy and observances of the Church, but to restrict Englishmen to a thorough conformity to the letter of the Prayer Book. The 1559 Prayer Book was not only necessary, it was sufficient. Thus the wide penumbra of Puritan practices and observances which had grown up around the Prayer Book was to be curtailed or abolished. This programme incensed all Puritans and worried most others. Just as bad was Laud's clericism, his attempt to restore the power and authority of the bishops, of the Church courts, and of the parish clergy by attacking lay encroachments on the wealth and jurisdiction of the Church. Church lands were to be restored, lay control of tithes and of clerical appointments restricted, and the clergy's power to enforce the laws of God enhanced. The most notable visual effect of Laud's archiepiscopate was the removal of the communion tables from the body of the church to the east end, where they were placed on a dais and railed off. At the same time, the rich and ornamental pews set up by the status-conscious clergy were to be removed and replaced by plain, unadorned ones. In the house of God the priest stood at the altar raised above the laity, who were to sit in awed humility beneath his gaze. Sinful man could not come to salvation through the word of God alone, or at all, but only through the sacraments mediated by God's priesthood. Only a priesthood freed from the greed and cloying materialism of the laity could carry out the Church's mission. Such a programme committed Laud to taking on almost every vested secular interest in the State.

Blunders Leading to Civil War

Despite this, as I have said, in 1637 Charles stood at the height of his power. Yet five years later civil war broke out. Only a catastrophic series of blunders made this possible. The most obvious lesson the king should have learnt from the 1620s (if not the 1590s) was that the Tudor–Stuart system of government was ill-equipped to fight successful wars, with or without parliamentary help. This did not matter since no one was likely to make war on England in the foreseeable future, giving the Crown time in an increasingly favourable economic climate (the great inflation petering out and foreign trade booming). What Charles had to avoid was blundering into an unnecessary war. In 1637, however, he blundered into civil war with his Scots subjects. Governing Scotland from London had proved beyond Charles, whose desire for order and conformity led him first to challenge the autonomy of the Scots lords in matters of jurisdiction and titles to secularized Church lands, and then to attempt to introduce religious reforms into Scotland similar to those advocated by Laud in England. Protests over the latter led to a collapse of order, and the king's alternating bluster and half-hearted concession led to a rapid escalation of the troubles. Within 12 months, Charles was faced by the ruin of his Scottish religious policies and an increasing challenge to his political authority there. He therefore decided to impose his will by force. In 1639 and again in 1640 he planned to invade Scotland. On both occasions the Scots mobilized more quickly, more thoroughly, and in greater numbers than he did. Rather than accept a deal with the Short Parliament (April–May 1640), which was willing to fund a campaign against the Scots in return for painful but feasible concessions (certainly for less than the Scots were demanding), Charles preferred to rely on

Irish Catholics, Highland Catholics, and specious offers of help from Spain and the Papacy. Poor co-ordination, poor morale, and a general lack of urgency both forced Charles to abandon the campaign of 1639 and allowed the Scots to invade England and to occupy Newcastle in the autumn of 1640. There they sat, refusing to go home until the king had made a treaty with them, including a settlement of their expenses, ratified by an English Parliament.

A unique opportunity thus arose for all those unhappy with royal policies to put things right: a Parliament was called which could not be dismissed at will. The ruthlessness of the way the opportunity was taken was largely the result of that unique circumstance. Within 12 months those institutions and prerogatives through which Charles had sustained his non-parliamentary government were swept away. The men who had counselled the king in the 1630s were in prison, in exile, or in disgrace. But the expected return to peace and co-operation did not occur. Instead, the crisis rapidly deepened amidst ever greater distrust and recrimination. Civil war itself broke out within two years to the dismay and bewilderment of almost everyone. The reasons why Charles's position collapsed so completely, so quickly, and so surprisingly are necessarily a matter of dispute amongst historians. But two points stand out. One is that once the constitutional reforms which were widely desired were achieved, Charles's palpable bad grace, his obvious determination to reverse his concessions at the earliest opportunity, and his growing willingness to use force to that end, drove the leaders of the Commons, and above all John Pym, to contemplate more radical measures. In 1640 almost without exception the members favoured a negative, restrained programme, the abolition of those powers, those prerogatives, and those courts which had sustained non-parliamentary government. No one had intended to increase the powers of the two Houses, but only to insist that Parliament be allowed to meet regularly to discharge its ancient duties: to make law, to grant supply, to draw the king's attention to the grievances of the subjects, and to seek redress. By the autumn of 1641 a wholly new view had emerged. It was that the king himself was so irresponsible, so incorrigible, that Parliament, on the people's behalf, had a right to transfer to themselves powers previously exercised by the king. Specifically, this meant that the Houses should play a part in the appointment and dismissal of privy councillors and principal officials of State and court, and that the Privy Council's debates and decisions should be subject to parliamentary scrutiny. Such demands were facilitated by the fact that Charles had made very similar concessions to the Scots in his treaty with them in July 1641, and the demands were given new urgency by the outbreak of the Irish rebellion in October.

The Catholics of the north of Ireland, fearful that the English Parliament would introduce new, repressive religious legislation, decided to take pre-emptive action to disarm those Ulster Protestants who would enforce any such legislation. With the legacy of hatred built into the Ulster plantations, violence inevitably got out of hand and something like 3,000 (that is, one in five) of the Protestants were slaughtered. Reports in England credibly suggested even larger numbers. Fatally for Charles I, the rebels claimed to be acting on his authority and produced a forged warrant to prove it. This reinforced rumours of Charles's scheming with Irish Catholics and of his negotiations with Catholic Spain and with the pope for men and money to invade Scotland in 1640, and it followed on from the discovery of army plots in England and Scotland earlier in the year to dissolve Parliament by force. Within weeks it was emphatically endorsed by Charles's attempt, with troops at his back, to arrest five members of the Commons during a sitting of the House. In these circumstances, to entrust Charles with recruiting and commanding the army to subjugate the Irish, an army available for service in England, was unthinkable. John Pym now led a parliamentary attack on Charles I as a deranged king, a man unfit to wield the powers of his office. In the 18 months before the outbreak of civil war, a majority of the Commons and a minority of the House of Lords came to share that conviction. When Charles I raised his standard at Nottingham and

declared war on his people, the question of his judgement and of his
trustworthiness was one which divided the nation.

The Outbreak of War

The first point about the outbreak of the war is, then, that Charles's
actions in 1640–2 forced many into a much more radical constitutional
position than they had taken or anticipated taking. But the
constitutional dynamic was a limited one. The question of trust arose in
relation to an urgent non-negotiable issue: the control of the armed
forces to be used against the Irish rebels. This turned attention on a
further, related question, the king's control of the militia and of those
who ran it, the lords-lieutenant and their deputies. These constitutional
issues together with the accountability of the king's ministers and
councillors to Parliament proved to be the occasion of the Civil War. But
they were not the prime considerations in the minds of those who
actively took sides. Certainly the question of trust drew some men to
the side of the Houses; but the palpably new demands now being made
by Pym and his colleagues were wholly unacceptable to many others. If
the king's flirtations with popery drove some into the arms of Pym, so
Pym drove others into the arms of the king by his reckless willingness to
use mass picketing by thousands of Londoners to intimidate wavering
members of both Houses to approve controversial measures. But for
every one who took sides on the constitutional issue in 1642, there were
ten who found it impossible to take sides, who saw right and wrong on
both sides, and who continued to pray and to beg for accommodation
and a peaceful settlement. In a majority of shires and boroughs, the
dominant mood throughout 1642 was pacifist, neutralist, or at least
localist. That is, attempts were made to neutralize whole regions, for
demilitarization agreements to be reached between factions or to be
imposed by 'peace' movements on both sides, or for the county
establishments to impose order and discipline in the name of king or
Parliament but without doing anything to further the larger, national
war effort. Constitutional issues, however much they pressed upon

those at Westminster who experienced royal duplicity and the London apprentices' politics of menace, were not in themselves weighty enough to start a civil war.

By 1642, however, a second factor was crucial: religion. The religious experiments of Archbishop Laud reactivated Puritan militancy. By 1640 substantial numbers of clergy, of gentry, and especially of prosperous farmers and craftsmen had decided that the system of Church government, so easily manipulated by a clique of innovators and crypto-Catholics such as they deemed the Laudians to be, had to be overthrown. The office of bishop must be abolished, the Prayer Book, which, said some, 'is noisome and doth stink in the nostrils of God', must be suppressed, and the observance of 'popish' festivals such as Christmas and Easter must be stopped. A majority in Parliament initially favoured a more moderate reform – the punishment of Laud and his henchmen, and legislation to reduce the autonomy and jurisdiction of the bishops. But the Scots' pressure for more change, a carefully orchestrated petitioning campaign for reform of the Church 'root and branch', and outbreaks of popular iconoclasm (the smashing of stained glass and the hacking out of communion rails were reported from many regions) led to a rapid polarization of opinion. Since many of those who campaigned against bishops also campaigned against rapacious landlords and against tithes (with implications for property rights in general), the defence of the existing Church became a defence of order and hierarchy in society and the State as well as in religion.

There was an Anglican party before there was a royalist party, and those who rushed to join the king in 1642 were those clearly motivated by religion. On the other side, those who mobilized for Parliament were those dedicated to the overthrow of the existing Church, and to the creation of a new evangelical Church which gave greater priority to preaching God's word and to imposing moral and social discipline. It was a vision reinforced by the return of exiles from New England who told of the achievements of the godly in the Wilderness. Like the

Israelites of the Old Testament led out of bondage in Egypt to the Promised Land, so God's new chosen people, the English, were to be led out of bondage into a Promised Land, a Brave New World. While the majority of the English dithered and compromised, the minority who took up the armed struggle cared passionately about religion.

Those who hesitated were, then, sucked inexorably into the Civil War. Faced by escalating demands and threats from the minority who had seized the initiative, most people had to choose sides. Many, maybe most, followed the line of least resistance and did what they were told by those in a position immediately to compel obedience. Others, deciding reluctantly and miserably, examined their consciences and then moved themselves and their families to an area under the control of the side which they thought the more honourable. But fear of the king's 'popish' allies and of Parliament's religious zealots made that decision unbearable for many.

Chapter 4
The Civil Wars

The First Civil War

The first Civil War lasted from 1642 until 1646. It is impossible to say quite when it began: the country drifted into war. In January 1642 the king left London and began a long journey round the Midlands and the north. In April he tried to secure an arsenal of military equipment at Hull (left over from his Scottish campaign). The gates were locked against him and he retired to York. Between June and August, Charles and the two Houses issued flatly contradictory instructions to rival groups of commissioners for the drilling of the militia. This led to some skirmishing and shows of force. By the end of August both sides were recruiting in earnest and skirmishing increased. The king's raising of his standard at Nottingham on 20 August was the formal declaration of war. But the hope on all sides remained either that negotiations would succeed or else that one battle between the two armies now in the making would settle the issue. But that first battle, at Edgehill in South Warwickshire on 23 October, was drawn and settled nothing. Although the king advanced on London and reached Brentford, he did not have the numbers or the logistical support to take on the forces blocking his path. He retreated to Oxford as the winter closed in and the roads became impassable. Only after a winter of fitful peace and futile negotiation did the real war break out. Those first armies had been cobbled together and paid on a hand-to-mouth basis. By the spring, it was clear that the nation had to be mobilized. Armies had to be raised in every region and the money and administrative apparatus to sustain those armies created. The country may have stumbled into war; but the logic of that war and its costs would turn civil disturbance into bloody revolution.

It is probable that at some moments in 1643–5 more than one in ten of all adult males was in arms. No single army exceeded 20,000 men, and the largest single battle – Marston Moor near York in June 1644, which saw the conjunction of several separate armies – involved fewer than 45,000 men. But there were usually 120,000 and up to 140,000 men in arms during the campaigning seasons of 1643, 1644, and 1645. Both sides organized themselves regionally into 'associations' of counties, each with an army (at least on paper) whose primary duty was to clear the association of enemies and to protect it from invasion. Both sides also had a 'marching army' with national responsibilities. In these circumstances the war was essentially one of skirmishes and sieges rather than of major battles. Some regions saw little fighting (for example, East Anglia, the south coast, mid-Wales); others were constantly marched over and occupied by rival armies (the Severn and Thames valleys were amongst the worst, but the whole of the Midlands was a constant military zone). Parliament's heartland was the area in the immediate vicinity of London. Proximity to the capital and to the peremptory demands of the Houses, and the rapid deployment of thousands of Londoners in arms (the unemployed and the religiously inclined joining up in uncertain proportions), ensured that the lukewarm and the hesitant accepted parliamentary authority. Equally, the king's initial strength lay in the areas he visited and toured: the North and East Midlands in a swathe of counties from Lancashire to Oxfordshire. The far north and the west were initially neutral or confused. Only gradually did royalists gain the upper hand in those areas.

Parliament's Advantages

The king had several initial advantages – the support of personally wealthy men, a naturally unified command structure emanating from the royal person, and a simpler military objective (to capture London). But Parliament had greater long-term advantages: the wealth and manpower of London, crucial for the provision of credit; the control of the navy and of the trade routes with the result that hard-headed businessmen preferred to deal with them rather than with the king; a greater compactness of territory less vulnerable to invasion than the royalist hinterlands; and the limited but important help afforded by the invasion of 20,000 Scots in 1644 in return for a commitment by the Houses to introduce a form of Church government similar to the Scottish one.

It was always likely that the parliamentary side would wear down the royalists in a long war. So it proved. Purely military factors played little part in the outcome. Both sides deployed the same tactics and used similar weapons; both had large numbers of experienced officers who had served in the armies of the Continental powers in the Thirty Years War. In 1645 both sides 'new modelled' their military organizations to take account of the changing military balance, the king setting up separate grand commands in Bristol and Oxford, Parliament bringing together three separate armies depleted in recent months: an army too large for its existing task, the defence of East Anglia, the unsuccessful southern region army of Sir William Waller, and the 'marching army' of the commander-in-chief, the earl of Essex. This New Model Army was put under the command of an 'outsider', Sir Thomas Fairfax, to avoid the rival claims of senior officers in the old armies, and all MPs were recalled from their commands to serve in the Houses; but otherwise commands were allocated more or less according to existing seniority. The New Model was not, by origin, designed to radicalize the parliamentary cause and it was not dominated by radical officers. Professionalization, not radicalization, was the key; the army's later reputation for religious zeal and for representing a career open to the talents was not a feature of its creation. The great string of victories beginning at Naseby in June 1645 was the product not of its zeal, but of regular pay. In the last 18 months of the war, the unpaid royalist armies simply dissolved, while the New Model was well supplied. The Civil War was won by attrition.

The last 12 months of the war saw a growing popular revolt against its violence and destruction. These neutralist or 'Clubmen' risings of farmers and rural craftsmen throughout west and south-west England sought to drive one or both sides out of their area, and demanded an end to the war by negotiation. Again, as the discipline of royalist armies disintegrated, they were the principal sufferers. But the hostility of the populace to both sides made the fruits of victory hard to pick.

Impositions on Pocket and Conscience

To win the war, Parliament had imposed massive taxation on the people. Direct taxation was itself set at a level of 15–20 per cent of the income of the rich and of the middling sort. Excise duties were imposed on basic commodities such as beer (the basic beverage of men, women, and children in an age just prior to the introduction of hot vegetable drinks such as tea, coffee, and chocolate) and salt (a necessary preservative in that period). Several thousand gentry and many thousands of others whose property lay in an area controlled by their opponents had their estates confiscated and their incomes employed wholly by the State, except for a meagre one-fifth allowed to those with wives and children. By the end of the war, Parliament was allowing less active royalists ('delinquents') to regain their estates on payment of a heavy fine; but the hardliners ('malignants') were allowed no redress and were later to suffer from the sale of their lands on the open market to the highest bidder. All those whose estates were not actually confiscated were required to lend money to king or Parliament; refusal to lend 'voluntarily' led to a stinging fine. In addition to those burdens,

Map 1. Major battles and sieges of the English Civil Wars, 1642–51

both sides resorted to free quarter, the billeting of troops on civilians with little prospect of any recompense for the board and lodging taken. Troops on the move were all too likely to help themselves and to point their muskets at anyone who protested. Looting and pillaging were rare; pilfering and trampling down crops were common. All this occurred in an economy severely disrupted by war. Trade up the Severn was seriously affected by the royalist occupation of Worcester and parliamentarian occupation of Gloucester; that up the Thames by royalist Oxford and parliamentarian Reading. Bad weather added to other problems to make the harvests of the later 1640s the worst of the century. High taxation and high food prices depressed the markets for manufactures and led to economic recession. The plight of the poor and of the not-so-poor was desperate indeed. The costs of settlement, of the disbandment of armies, and of a return to 'normality' grew.

Parliament also had to grant extensive powers, even arbitrary powers, to its agents. The war was administered by a series of committees in London that oversaw the activities of committees in each county and regional association. Committees at each level were granted powers quite at variance with the principles of common law: powers to assess people's wealth and impose their assessments; to search premises and to distrain goods; and to imprison those who obstructed them without trial, without cause shown, and without limitation. Those who acted in such roles were granted an indemnity against any civil or criminal action brought against them, and (after mid-1647) that indemnity was enforced by another parliamentary committee. Judgements reached in the highest courts of the land were set aside by committee decree. Only thus had the resources to win the Civil War been secured. But by 1647 and 1648 Parliament was seen as being more tyrannical in its government than the king had been in his. The cries for settlement and restoration were redoubled.

In addition, Parliament promised the Scots that the Elizabethan Church would be dismantled and refashioned 'according to the word of God, and the example of the best reformed churches' (a piece of casuistry, since the Scots wrongly assumed that must mean their own Church). By 1646 this was accomplished, on paper at least. Episcopacy, cathedrals, Church courts, the Book of Common Prayer, and the Calendar (including the celebration of Christmas and Easter) were abolished and proscribed. In their place a 'Presbyterian' system was set up. Ministers and lay 'elders' from a group of neighbouring churches were to meet monthly to discuss matters of mutual concern. Representatives of all such meetings or 'classes' within each county were to meet regularly. The activities at parish, classical, and provincial level would be co-ordinated by a national synod and by Parliament. No one was exempt from the authority of this new national Church any more than they had been from that of the old Church. The new national faith would be based upon a new service book ('the Directory of Public Worship', emphasizing extempore prayer and the preaching of the Word), new catechisms, and new articles of faith. At every level, the 'godly' were to be empowered to impose moral duties, a 'reformation of manners', and strict spiritual observance through ecclesiastical and secular sanctions. But this Puritan experiment was stillborn. It gave the laity far too much control to please many strict Presbyterian ministers. It gave too little authority to the individual parishes and too much to classes, provinces, and synods to please many others. The precise doctrinal, liturgical, and disciplinary requirements were too rigid for others or just plain unacceptable in themselves. While there was 'Puritan' unity in 1642 against the existing order, the imposition of one particular alternative created a major split in the movement. Many 'Independents' refused to accept the package and began to demand liberty of conscience for themselves and a right of free religious assembly outside the national Church. Some began to refuse to pay tithes. The disintegration of Puritanism preceded any attempt to impose the Presbyterian system. At the same time, this system was bitterly opposed by the great majority of ordinary people. Over four generations they had come to love the Prayer Book and the celebration of the great Christian festivals. They resented the loss of both, and also the Puritan doctrine that forbade anyone to come to receive holy communion without first being approved by the minister and his self-righteous henchmen and given a certificate of worthiness. Throughout much of England, therefore, including East Anglia, the decrees against the Prayer Book and the celebration of festivals were a dead letter. Ministers who tried to impose change were opposed and even thrown out, and although one in five of the clergy were ejected by parliamentary commissions for spiritual, moral, or political unfitness, a majority of their replacements sought secret episcopal ordination. The Puritan experiment was ineffective but added to popular hatred of an arbitrary Parliament.

Radical Beliefs

But if the great majority, even on the winning side, became convinced that the Civil War had solved nothing and had only substituted new and harsher impositions on pocket and conscience for the old royal impositions, a minority, equally dismayed by the shabby realities of the present, persuaded themselves that a much more radical transformation of political institutions was necessary. God could not have subjected his people to such trials and sufferings without a good purpose. To admit the futility of the struggle, to bring back the king on terms he would have accepted in 1642, would be a betrayal of God and of those who had died and suffered in His cause. Once again it was the religious imperative which drove men on. Such views were to be found in London, with its concentration of gathered churches and economic distress, and in the army, with its especially strong memories of suffering and exhilaration, many soldiers being aware of God's presence with them in the heat of battle. Furthermore a penniless Parliament, bleakly foreseeing the consequences of seeking to squeeze additional taxes from the people, enraged the army in the spring of 1647 by trying to disband most of it and to send the rest to reconquer Ireland without paying off the arrears of pay which had been mounting since the end of the war. In the summer of 1647 and again in the autumn of 1648 a majority in the two Houses, unable to see the way forward, resigned themselves to accepting such terms as the king would accept. His plan since his military defeat, to keep talking but to keep his options open, looked likely to be vindicated.

On both occasions, however, the army prevented Parliament from surrender. In August 1647 it marched into London, plucked out the leading 'incendiaries' from the House of Commons, and awed the rest into voting it the taxation and the other material comforts it believed due to it. In doing so, the army spurned the invitation of the London-based radical group known as the Levellers to dissolve the Long Parliament, to decree that all existing government had abused its trust and was null and void, and to establish a new democratic constitution. The Levellers wanted all free-born Englishmen to sign a social contract, an Agreement of the People, and to enjoy full rights of participation in a decentralized, democratic state. All those who held office would do so for a very short period and were to be accountable to their constituents. Many rights, above all freedom to believe and practise whatever form of Christianity one wanted, could not be infringed by any future Parliament or government. The army, officers and men, were drawn to the Levellers' commitment to religious freedom and to their condemnation of the corruption and tyranny of the Long Parliament, and officers and 'agitators' drawn from the rank and file debated Leveller proposals, above all at the Putney debates held in and near Putney church in November 1647. But the great majority finally decided that the army's bread-and-butter demands were not to be met by those proposals. Instead the army preferred to put pressure on the chastened Parliament to use its arbitrary powers to meet their sectional interests.

The Second Civil War

The outcome was a second Civil War, a revolt of the provinces against centralization and military rule. Moderate parliamentarians, Clubmen, and whole county communities rose against the renewed oppressions, and their outrage was encouraged and focused by ex-royalists. The second Civil War was fiercest in regions little affected by the first war, insufficiently numbed by past experience – in Kent, in East Anglia, in South Wales, in the West and North Ridings. It was complicated by the king's clumsy alliance with the Scots, who were disgusted by Parliament's failure to honour its agreement to bring in a Church settlement like their own, and who were willing, despite everything, to trust in vague assurances from the duplicitous Charles. If the revolts had been co-ordinated, or at least contemporaneous, they might have succeeded. But they happened one by one, and one by one the army picked them off. With the defeat of the Scots at Preston in August, the second Civil War was over.

It had solved nothing. Still the country cried out for peace and for settlement, still the army had to be paid, still the king prevaricated and made hollow promises. As in 1647, the Houses had to face the futility of all their efforts. By early December there were only two alternatives: to capitulate to the king and to bring him back on his own terms to restore order and peace; or to remove him, and to launch on a bold adventure into unknown and uncharted constitutional seas. A clear majority of both Houses, and a massive majority of the country, wanted the former; a tiny minority, spearheaded by the leaders of the army, determined on the latter. For a second time the army purged Parliament. In the so-called Pride's Purge, over half the members of the Commons were arrested or forcibly prevented from taking their seats. Two-thirds of the remainder boycotted the violated House. In the revolutionary weeks that followed, fewer than one in six of all MPs participated, and many of those in attendance did so to moderate proceedings. The decision to put the king on trial was probably approved by fewer than one in ten of the assembly that had made war on him in 1642.

Trial and Execution

In January 1649, the king was tried for his life. His dignity and forbearance made it a massive propaganda defeat for his opponents. His public beheading at Whitehall took place before a stunned but sympathetic crowd. This most dishonourable and duplicitous of English kings grasped a martyr's crown, his reputation rescued by that dignity at the end and by the publication of his self-justification, the *Eikon Basilike*, a runaway best-seller for decades to come.

Chapter 5
Commonwealth and
Protectorate

From 1649 to 1660 England was a republic. In some ways this was a revolutionary period indeed. Other kings had been brutally murdered, but none had previously been legally murdered. Monarchy was abolished, along with the House of Lords and the Anglican Church. England had four separate constitutions between 1649 and 1659, and a chaos of expedients in 1659–60. Scotland was fully integrated into Britain, and Ireland subjugated with an arrogance unprecedented even in its troubled history. It was a period of major experiment in national government. Yet a remarkable amount was left untouched. The legal system was tinkered with but was recognizably the old, arcane common law system run by an exclusive legal priesthood; local government reverted to the old pattern as quarter sessions returned to constitute veritable local parliaments. Exchequer reasserted its control over government finance. Existing rights of property were protected and reinforced, and the social order defended from its radical critics. There was a loosely structured national Church. If no one was obliged to attend this national Church, all were required to pay tithes to support its clergy and to accept the secular and moral authority of parish officers in the execution of the duties laid upon them in Tudor statutes. In practice, the very freedom allowed to each parish in matters of worship, witness, and observance permitted Anglican services and the Anglican feasts to be quietly and widely practised.

The Rump

Institutionally, it was indeed a decade of uneven progress back towards a restoration of monarchy. From 1649 to 1653, England was governed by the Rump Parliament, that fragment of the Long Parliament which accepted Pride's Purge and the regicide and which assumed unto itself all legislative and executive power. Despite the high-minded attempts of some MPs to liken themselves to the assemblies of the Roman republic, the Rump in practice was a body that lived from hand to mouth. Too busy to take bold initiatives and to seek long-term solutions, let alone to build the new Jerusalem, the Rump fended off its problems. By selling the Crown's lands, Church lands, and royalist lands, it financed the army's conquest of Ireland – which included the storming of Drogheda and Wexford and the slaughtering of the civilian population, acts unparalleled in England, but justified as revenge for the massacres of 1641 – and its gentler invasion of Scotland. By the establishment of extra-parliamentary financial institutions and by the restoration of pre-war forms of local government, the Rump wooed enough men in the provinces into acquiescence to keep going and to defeat the royalists in a third Civil War. By incoherent and contradictory pronouncements on religion, it kept most men guessing about its ecclesiastical priorities, and drove none to desperate opposition. The Rump even blundered into a naval war with the Dutch and captured enough Dutch merchantmen in the ensuing months to double Britain's entrepôt trade. A demoralized royalist party licked its wounds and tried to pay off its debts; a dejected majority of the old parliamentarian party grudgingly did what they were told but little more. The Rump stumbled on.

By the spring of 1653 the army was ready for a change. With fresh testimonies of divine favour in its victories in Scotland and Ireland and over Charles II at the battle of Worcester, its leaders, above all its commander (since 1649) Oliver Cromwell, demanded the kind of godly

6. Oliver Cromwell on the eve of his brutal and victorious campaign in Ireland, 1649–50

reformation which the Rump was too preoccupied and too set in its ways to institute.

Barebones Parliament

Disagreements between Rumpers and army commanders led finally to the peremptory dissolution which the latter had ducked in 1647 and 1648. Fearful that free elections would provoke a right-wing majority, Cromwell decided to call an 'assembly of saints', a constituent assembly of 140 hand-picked men drawn from amongst those who had remained loyal to the godly cause, men who shared little beyond having what Cromwell called 'the root of the matter in them', an integrity and intensity of experience of God's purpose for his people, whose task it was to institute a programme of moral regeneration and political education that Cromwell hoped would bring the people to recognize and to own the 'promises and prophecies' of God. Cromwell's vision of 140 men with a fragment to contribute to the building up of a mosaic of truth was noble but naive. These 140 bigots of the Nominated or Barebones Parliament, leaderless and without co-ordination, bickered for five months and then, by a large majority, surrendered their power back into the lord general's hands. Cromwell's honest attempts to persuade others to govern while he stood aside had failed. The army alone propped up the republic and could make and break governments. The army must be made responsible for governing.

Lord Protector Cromwell

From December 1653 until his death in September 1658, Oliver Cromwell ruled England as lord protector and head of state. Under two paper constitutions, the *Instrument of Government* (1653–7, issued by the Army Council) and the *Humble Petition and Advice* (1657–8, drawn up by Parliament), Cromwell as head of the executive had to rule with, and through, a Council of State. He also had to meet Parliament regularly. Cromwell saw himself in a position very similar to that of Moses leading the Israelites to the Promised Land. The English people had been in bondage in the Land of Egypt (Stuart monarchy); they had fled and crossed the Red Sea (regicide); they were now struggling across the Desert (current misfortunes), guided by the Pillar of Fire (divine providence manifested in the army's great victories, renewed from 1655 on in a successful war against Spain). The people, like the Israelites, were recalcitrant and complaining. Sometimes they needed to be frog-marched towards the Promised Land, as in 1655-6 when Cromwell became dismayed by the lack of response in the people at large during an abortive royalist uprising (few royalists participated but many turned a blind eye, and few beyond the army rushed to extinguish the flames of rebellion). He then instituted a system of government placing each region under the supervision of a senior military commander. These 'Major Generals' were responsible for security but also interfered in every aspect of local government and instituted a 'reformation of manners' (a campaign of moral rearmament). At other times Cromwell tried to wheedle the nation towards the Promised Land with policies of 'healing and settling', playing down the power of the sword and attempting to broaden participation in government and to share power with local magistrates and with Parliament.

If Cromwell had settled for acquiescence and a minimum level of political acceptance, he could have established a secure and lasting regime. But he yearned for commitment and zeal, for a nation more responsive to the things of God, more willing to obey God's commands. Cromwell was an orthodox Calvinist in his belief in the duty of God's elect to make all men love and honour Him, and in his belief that divine providence showed God's people the way forward. Cromwell was unusual in believing that, in this fallen world, the elect were scattered amongst the Churches. Toleration was a means to the end of restoring the unity of God's word and truth. This religious radicalism went along with a social conservatism. The hierarchical ordering of society was natural and good, its flaws and injustices not intrinsic but the consequence of sin. It was not society but human behaviour within society that must be reformed.

By executing Charles, Cromwell cut himself off from justifications of political authority rooted in the past; by acknowledging that a free vote of those who held the franchise would restore the king, that is by refusing to base his authority on consent, Cromwell cut himself off from arguments of the present. His self-justification lay in the future, in the belief that he was fulfilling God's will. But because he believed that he had such a task to perform, he had a fatal disregard for civil and legal liberties. To achieve the future promised by God, Cromwell governed arbitrarily. He imprisoned men without trial. When George Cony, a merchant, refused to pay unconstitutional customs duties, Cromwell imprisoned him and his lawyer to prevent him taking his case to court. When Parliament failed to make him an adequate financial provision, he taxed by decree. When the people would not respond voluntarily to the call to moral regeneration, he created major generals and set them to work. Hence the supreme paradox. Cromwell the king-killer, the reluctant head of State, the visionary, was begged by his second Parliament to become King Oliver. He was offered the Crown. Ironically he was offered it to limit his power, to bind him with precedents and with the rule of law. Because such restrictions were irrelevant to the task he believed he was entrusted to perform, because God's Providence did not direct him to restore the office that He had set aside, he declined the throne.

While Cromwell lived, the army (who had the immediate military muscle) and the country gentry (who had the ultimate social authority) were kept in creative tension. Cromwell was a unique blend of country gentleman and professional soldier, of religious radical and social conservative, of political visionary and constitutional mechanic, of charismatic personal presence and insufferable self-righteousness. He was at once the only source of stability and the ultimate source of instability of the regimes he ran. If he could have settled for settlement, he could have established a prudent republic; if he had not had a fire in his belly to change the world, he would never have risen from sheep farmer to be head of state. With his death, the republic collapsed. His son lacked his qualities and succumbed to the jealousy of the senior military commanders. They in turn fell out amongst themselves and a national tax strike hastened the disintegration of the army. Eighteen months after Oliver Cromwell's death, one section of the army under General Monck decided that enough was enough. Free elections were held and Charles II was recalled.

Chapter 6
Restoration Monarchy

Charles was restored unconditionally. His reign was declared to have
begun at the moment of his father's death; those Acts of Parliament to
which his father had assented were in force, all the rest were null and
void (which meant, for example, that all Crown and Church land sold off
by the republic was restored, but also that those royalists who had paid
fines or who had repurchased their estates under Commonwealth
legislation went uncompensated). Parliament assured itself of no
greater role in the government than it had possessed under Elizabeth
and the early Stuarts (except for a toothless act requiring a triennial
session of Parliament, an Act Charles II ignored without popular protest
in 1684). Since the Long Parliament and those of the interregnum had
abused their authority as freely as Charles I had done, it seemed
pointless to build them up as a counterpoise to the Crown. Rather, the
Restoration settlement sought to limit royal power by handing power
back from the centre to the localities.

The Settlement

Charles I had agreed to the abolition of the prerogative courts, to the
restriction of the judicial power of the Privy Council (now emasculated
and thus unable to enforce policy), and to the abolition of prerogative
taxation. The local gentry were freer than ever before to run their own
shires. What is more, with remarkable nerve and courage, Charles set

out to build his regime on as broad a base as possible. He refused to give special positions of favour and trust to his own and his father's friends. There was to be power-sharing at every level of government: in the council and in the distribution of office at court, in the bureaucracy, and in local government. Old royalists, old parliamentarian moderates who had shunned the interregnum regimes, and Cromwellian loyalists, all found places. Indeed, the group who did least well were the royalist exiles. Charles defeated parliamentary attempts at a wide proscription and punishment of the enemies of monarchy. Only those who signed Charles I's death warrant and a handful of others were exempted from the general Act of Indemnity and Oblivion (one bitter cavalier called the Restoration an 'act of indemnity to the King's enemies and of oblivion to his friends'). It took courage to determine that it was better to upset old friends (who would not send the king on his travels again) than to upset old enemies. Plots against Charles II were few and restricted to radical religious sects. Even a government with fewer than 3,000 men in arms could deal with such threats.

Charles had hoped to bring a similar comprehensiveness to the ecclesiastical settlement. He sought to restore the Church of England, but with reforms that would make it acceptable to the majority of moderate Puritans. To this end, he offered bishoprics to a number of such moderates and he issued an interim settlement (the Worcester House Declaration) which weakened the power and autonomy of the bishops and made the more contentious ceremonies and phrases of the Prayer Book optional. He also wanted to grant freedom of religious assembly (if not equality of political rights) to the tiny minority of Puritans and Catholics who could not accept even a latitudinarian national Church. For 18 months he fought for this moderate settlement, only to be defeated by the determination of the rigorist Anglican majority in the Cavalier Parliament, by the luke-warmness of his advisers, and by the self-destructive behaviour of Richard Baxter and the Puritan leaders. They refused the senior positions in the Church offered them, they campaigned against toleration, and they persisted in unreasonable demands at the conference held to reform the Prayer Book. Their Scottish colleagues, more flexible and pragmatic, achieved a settlement acceptable to a majority of their brethren.

Charles finally abandoned the quest for a comprehensive Church and assented to the Act of Uniformity, which restored the old Church, lock, stock, and barrel, and which imposed a number of stringent oaths and other tests on the clergy. In consequence about one in five of the clergy were ejected by the end of 1662, and many of them began to set up conventicles outside the Church. Charles then set about promoting the cause of religious toleration for all non-Anglicans. Even though his first attempt in January 1663 was a failure, he had the consolation of knowing that he had reversed traditional roles. The pre-war Puritans had looked to Parliament for protection from the king; the new nonconformists had to look to him for protection from Parliament. For 15 years this made his position in relation to the majority of them politically safe. Nonetheless, it was the single greatest weakness of the Restoration settlement. A comprehensive political settlement was set against a narrow, intolerant religious one. Few local governors were Dissenters; but many were sympathetic to them and reluctant to impose the full strictures of the vindictive laws which Parliament went on to pass against their religious assemblies.

Lines of Policy

In general, Charles's problems arose not from the settlement but from his preferred lines of policy. In some ways, he was a lazy king. His adolescence and early manhood had been dominated by the desire to gain the throne, and once he had returned from exile all his ambition was spent. He was the only one of the Stuarts not to be a visionary, not to have long-term goals. This made it easy for him to back down whenever his policies were strongly opposed. But while he lacked vision, he did not lack prejudices and preferences. He was a man with a strong rationalist streak – a worldly man with many mistresses and 17

7. Barbara Villiers, countess of Castlemaine, rather smugly holds up one of her four bastards by Charles II. Altogether Charles acknowledged 17 bastards, but he rarely kept more than one mistress at once

acknowledged bastards, a cynic with regard to human nature, and an intellectual dilettante who took a lively if spasmodic interest in the affairs of the Royal Society launched at his accession. But this intellectual empiricism was joined with an emotional and spiritual mysticism which he got from his parents. He believed that he possessed semi-divine powers and attributes (no king touched so much for the king's evil, that class of unpleasant glandular and scrofulous disorders that kings were reputed to be able to cure). He was also strongly drawn to Roman Catholicism. His mother, wife, brother, and favourite sister were all Catholics, and while he had a *bonhomie* which made him accessible to many, it was superficial, and he was only really close to his family. He knew that wherever Catholicism was strong, monarchy was strong. The Catholics had remained conspicuously loyal to his father. If any theology of grace made sense to Charles it was Catholic doctrine (of his mistresses, Charles said that he could not believe that God would damn a man for taking a little pleasure by the way). He was drawn to Catholicism and twice revealed that preference (in a secret treaty with France in 1670 and in his deathbed reception into the Catholic Church). He was much too sensible politically to declare himself except on his deathbed. But it did lead him to make clear his commitment to toleration. Both this and his obvious admiration for his cousin Louis XIV of France caused growing alarm in England.

Charles was given a generous financial settlement in 1660–1 (£1.2 million per annum), principally from indirect taxation. Bad housekeeping made this inadequate in his early years, and in general it left him with little flexibility. He had no ability to raise emergency taxation without recourse to Parliament and limited access to long-term credit. Although Charles had sole responsibility for foreign policy and for making war and peace, Parliament clearly would not vote the necessary revenues without a consideration of the cause for which the money was needed.

The period needed a great administrative reformer in the mould of Henry VIII's Thomas Cromwell, and it did not find one. Decision-making and policy enforcement needed restructuring and formalizing. The Council was too large and amorphous to be effective, and decisions were too often made at one *ad hoc* meeting in the king's chambers and unmade at a subsequent *ad hoc* meeting. This led to real uncertainty and eventually to panic about who was in charge. With the Council emasculated, enforcement of policy was left to individual ministers and departments without co-ordination. Patronage was chaotically handled. Equally, Parliament was inefficient and increasingly crotchety. Charles, feeling that those elected in 1661 were as loyal a group of royalists as he was likely to meet, kept the 'Cavalier' Parliament in almost annual sessions for 18 years. In part, its inefficiency was due to a growing rivalry between the two Houses, especially over the Lords' claim to take over much of the jurisdiction of the defunct conciliar courts, and a number of sessions were wrecked by deadlock on such issues. In part, its inefficiency was due to there being no government programme for it to get its teeth into. A body of several hundred members without recognized leadership spent much time discussing what to discuss. With most senior ministers in the Lords, and a predisposition to resist management by the court, the 1660s and 1670s were years of drift. Charles ruled without serious threat to his position at home or abroad. The early euphoria gave way to a mild political depression as the final ravages of plague, the humiliating Dutch incursions up the Medway during the second Dutch War (1665–7), and the Great Fire of London (1666) sapped the self-confidence of 1660–1 that God would bless a land that had come to its senses.

The Exclusion Crisis

There were many political embarrassments, such as the defeat of a major attempt to introduce religious toleration (1672–3), the suspension of interest payments on his loans (1672), and the political brawls in Parliament as the discredited ministers of the 'Cabal' administration blamed each other for their collective failure (1674–5). But the only challenge to his authority came in the Exclusion crisis of 1678–81. This

8. A pope-burning procession on 17 November 1680, commemorating the accession of Queen Elizabeth I

was triggered by the revelations of Titus Oates, Israel Tonge, and other desperadoes of a popish plot to murder Charles and put his Catholic brother on the throne. This was more lucid and more plausible than many similar tales, but was just as mendacious. The mysterious death of an investigating magistrate and the discovery of conspiratorial letters in the possession of James's private secretary also heightened tension. The result was a full-scale attempt to place a parliamentary bar on the accession of James and thereby to shatter Charles's divine-right theories of government.

In fact the political leaders of the Exclusion movement were at least as concerned to use the crisis to clip Charles's wings as James's. For the first 12 months their target was not James but Charles's Cavalier–Anglican chief minister, the earl of Danby. This appears odd, but it is clear that Shaftesbury, the leader of the Opposition, saw Danby's regime as just as much a threat to liberties as James might be. Danby's principles were the very antithesis of Shaftesbury's, in that he had developed sophisticated techniques of parliamentary management, had centralized financial control, had upset the balance of interests in local government to the advantage of Cavalier–Anglicans, seemed willing to develop a standing army in peacetime, and had allied with the Dutch against the French. Shaftesbury, a turncoat in the Civil War, a member of the Barebones Parliament and of Cromwell's Council of State, who had served Charles as chancellor of the Exchequer and lord chancellor, had a consistent record of supporting free and unfettered Parliaments, decentralization, and religious toleration, a horror of standing armies, and a distaste for the Dutch. Danby's policies amounted in fact to nothing more than a programme to give Charles II a quiet life: to Shaftesbury it looked like incipient absolutism. By now there was such a conjunction in people's minds between popery and arbitrary government that even Danby could be portrayed as a secret agent of the papists, despite his impeccable Anglicanism. Only when Danby was imprisoned in the Tower did Shaftesbury turn to Exclusion, as an end in itself and as a means to other ends. These included shattering the theoretical basis of divine right and creating the need for continued political action and cohesion (to secure Exclusion on Charles's death, for James would hardly accept it without a fight). To secure Exclusion, Shaftesbury created the first political party in English history. His 'Whigs' produced a mass of propaganda, organized petitions and demonstrations, and co-ordinated campaigns in three successive general elections (1679–81).

They failed. Charles held all the trump cards. The Whigs were fatally divided over who should take James's place as heir – Monmouth, the favoured royal bastard, or Mary, James's Protestant daughter. Almost without exception, the Whigs were committed to lawful, peaceful action only. The memories of civil war were too strong to allow violent councils to hold sway. Charles could, and did, use his power to summon and dissolve Parliament to his own advantage; he had a solid majority in the House of Lords that would vote down the Exclusion Bill time after time; a trade boom enhanced royal revenues on trade and freed Charles from financial worry; and his policy of offering concessions short of Exclusion bought off many moderates. Shaftesbury fatally assumed that Charles would weaken under pressure. He never grasped that Charles would always concede matters of policy, but never matters of principle. Charles would never have surrendered his divine right. His ultimate sacrifice would have been to divorce the barren queen he respected if he did not cherish, to remarry, and to solve the succession crisis via the marriage bed. It would have been the supreme demonstration of his political style.

As it was, the same iron nerve, pragmatism, and easy goodwill to all which he had demonstrated in 1660 won him the day. A nation racked by political deadlock for three years backed off, took stock, and rallied to him. In his last years he was able to pick off those who had crossed him, reward those who had stood by him, and enjoy a quiet life at last. He left a nation governed by and for those who believed in the divine right of kings, the divine right of the Church of England, and the divine right of the localities to run their own affairs. The complacency of the Tory–Anglicans knew no bounds, as they welcomed James II to the throne, the king whose rights they had protected. Such complacency was in for a rude shock.

James II

James was in fact a bigot. His government of Scotland in the early 1680s had seen a most severe repression and extensive use of judicial torture against Protestant Dissenters ('conventiclers'). Worse still, James believed himself to be a moderate. He had no deliberate plan to set himself up as an absolutist king on the Continental model. But since a trade boom greatly enhanced royal revenues (and his first Parliament, meeting under threat of a military bid for the throne by Charles's favoured bastard, the duke of Monmouth, voted higher rates in addition), he was able to maintain an army of 20,000 men. The army's most striking characteristic was its professionalism and the apolitical views of its career commanders. James had twice urged Charles to use his tiny army to get rid of troublesome Parliaments. He would not have hesitated to use his army against a recalcitrant assembly, but he did not intend to rule without Parliament. Indeed, at the time of his fall, he was engaged in the most elaborate operation ever attempted to 'pack' Parliament with sympathizers. Until early 1688 James's second marriage, more than a decade old, was childless. James – already 50 years old – expected to be succeeded by his Protestant daughter Mary and her Dutch husband, William of Orange. He intended to secure for all time a religious and civil equality for his co-religionists. This meant not only removing from them all the penalties and disabilities under the Penal Laws (fines for non-attendance at Anglican worship) and Test Acts (barring them from all offices and paid employments under the Crown), but also allowing the Catholic Church to be set up alongside the Anglican Church. This meant establishing a Catholic hierarchy and diocesan structure and public places of worship. It also meant allowing Catholics a share in the universities (maybe even the take-over – or

9. James II had a distinguished military and naval career blighted by his ignominious flight in 1688

'restoration' – of some colleges to serve as Catholic seminaries). It would probably have led on to granting Catholics exemption from tithes and the authority of Anglican courts. James honestly believed that once the ban on Catholic evangelism was lifted, once the civil and religious disabilities were removed, the return of hundreds of thousands to the Faith was certain. He believed that this granting of 'equal status' to Catholics was a humane and moderate programme. If, in the short term, a certain amount of positive discrimination was necessary to favour Catholics in appointments to national and local office, this too was only fair as a correcting exercise.

It need hardly be said that the Tory–Anglican political nation was outraged. Their loyalty to the Church proved greater than their loyalty to their anointed king. James soon discovered that no Tory–Anglican Parliament would repeal the anti-Catholic legislation and while a packed judiciary would uphold his suspension of that legislation, it would come back into force the moment he died and his Protestant heir took over. He therefore made a desperate bid to jettison the Tory squirearchy and to build an alternative power-base in an alliance of Catholics and Protestant Dissenters. Three-quarters of all JPs were sacked, together with most lords-lieutenant. The new men were of lower social origin, and James's purge constituted a greater social revolution in local government than had been attempted even in the years 1646–60. James called in the charters of most towns and reorganized their governments to give Dissenters control (this was especially vital if he was to get a sympathetic parliamentary majority). To win over the Dissenters, a Declaration of Indulgence was issued giving them full religious freedom.

The Tory–Anglicans were stung, but initially pacific. The whirlwind would blow itself out; James would die and Mary succeed him; they would take their revenge. Passive disobedience would limit James's success. Thus seven bishops petitioned him explaining why they would not obey his order to instruct their clergy to read the Declaration of Indulgence to their flocks. They also committed the Church to a future

72

Anglican toleration of Protestant dissenters. James had the bishops tried for seditious libel, but even his judges summed up against him and they were acquitted. Meanwhile, the Tory complacency of 1687 ('we are not to be laughed out of our doctrine of Non-Resistance and passive obedience on all occasions', wrote the marquis of Halifax) turned to stunned horror in June 1688 just as the trial got under way with the birth of a son and heir to James II. Now indeed the possibility of a dynasty of rabid Catholics appeared to stretch out before them.

Ironically, while many Anglican leaders came to put their religion before their political principles, many Dissenters chose to put political principles first. They had little doubt that James was using them for present purposes only. Thus leaders of both parties joined in the desperate expedient of inviting William of Orange to come to England, suitably protected with armed men, to remonstrate with James. Perhaps they really believed that this would lead to James agreeing to William's humiliating terms: the recall of the writ designed to produce a packed Parliament and new writs to return a 'free' Parliament; a declaration of war on France; and a commission to investigate the legitimacy of the infant Prince of Wales. Only a minority were willing to join William's invasion by taking up arms; but even fewer were willing to lift their little fingers to help James.

William III

Whatever those who invited William may have expected, William himself almost certainly intended to depose James. He was taking a quite outrageous risk, justified only by the necessity of harnessing the whole of Britain's military, naval, and financial resources to the struggle against Louis XIV. But how he expected to secure the throne is less clear. In the event, he was able to get himself proclaimed joint ruler with Mary within a matter of weeks because James had what can only be called a complete mental collapse. His army and William's never met. William landed at Torbay on 5 November and moved east. James brought his army as far as Salisbury, where incessant nosebleeds held him up. As his behaviour became more and more bizarre and manic, many of his professional officers and commanders deserted him. James then fled back to London and was quickly in William's hands. Even then, his position was not hopeless. A series of vague undertakings and promises would have ensured that he retained the loyalty of most peers and leading gentry. But he was beyond reason. He twice escaped (on the first occasion, to William's annoyance, being captured on the Kent coast by well-meaning fishermen and sent back). His flight to France, the public promises of Louis XIV to use French arms to restore him, and William's clear statement that he would not protect the realm unless he shared the throne with his wife left the political nation no choice. Almost all Whigs and most Tories, rationalizing their conduct as best they could, and in a variety of ways, agreed that James had vacated his throne and that the Crown be offered jointly to William and Mary. The Glorious Revolution of 1688 was even more unanticipated and unplanned than the Great Rebellion of 1642; its consequences probably more momentous.

Effects on the Crown

Had the English Revolution had any lasting effects on the power of the Crown? The answer is that it had surprisingly little. In the 1680s the Crown was far better endowed financially, it had a growing but still inadequate civil service, and it had an unprecedented opportunity to create a standing army. Parliaments had shown themselves quite unable to defeat the king, in the sense of imposing on him restrictions and conditions that he disliked or taking away from him powers he had hitherto enjoyed. The royal prerogatives in the 1650s were little different from those of the 1600s. The king could veto bills he did not approve; he could dispense individuals from the operation of statutes; and he could pardon whomsoever he chose. He selected his own councillors, judges, and senior administrators, and he could dismiss most of them at will. He was not bound to take anyone's advice. If he had lost most of his feudal revenues and his 'discretionary' powers to raise money, he had been amply compensated by parliamentary taxes, some in perpetuity, others for life.

The only really major weakening of royal power had come in the legislation of 1641 which abolished those courts and councils which were particularly susceptible to royal control. The most important restriction was the one which took away from the Privy Council its judicial power. Its teeth removed, the Council ceased to be an executive, active body, monitoring, cajoling, and directing the work of local government, and reverted to what it had begun as: a talking shop, a place where the king sought advice. It probably never functioned as well under the Stuarts as under the Tudors; James I allowed factionalism to spill over from the Council to the floor of Parliament; Charles I did not want to hear alternative proposals from groups within the Council. He wanted puppets to confirm his own preconceptions. Charles II enjoyed policymaking in secret, summoning ministers to hasty meetings in his private quarters, so that no one knew what was going on. For different reasons, each of these monarchs encouraged the growth of secret committees of the Council comprising the holders of key offices. Here was the seed of the Cabinet councils of the eighteenth century. Other conciliar courts abolished in 1641 included Star Chamber, High Commission, Requests, and – more by chance than design – the Regional Councils of the north and in the marches of Wales. Charles II was restricted at the Restoration not by the gentry in Parliament, but by the gentry in the provinces. Almost all the methods by which Tudor and early Stuart kings could bring recalcitrant county communities to heel had been taken away. Government was more than ever by their active consent. In the 1660s all taxation except the customs, all ecclesiastical legislation (such as the Act of Uniformity, the Conventicle Acts, and the Five Mile Act), and most security matters were entrusted to the gentry magistrates, with no appeal from their decisions to the central courts.

The abolition of the monarchy and the experience of republican rule thus had a very limited direct impact. Even the memory of Charles I's public trial, conviction, and decapitation did not change the monarchy's pretensions to rule by divine right or make it more respectful of Parliaments. After all, the political nation knew that regicide had cost them dear, that it had added to, rather than removed, their oppressions. The problems of matching resources to responsibilities had become clearer; but the problems themselves had neither increased nor diminished. The alternatives for England were to see either a strengthening of the central executive and administration at the expense of the independent county gentry; or else a further withering away of the centre, turning England into a series of semi-autonomous county states, self-governing, undertaxed, and stagnant. The latter was the preference of a range of 'Country parties' visible in the Parliaments of the 1620s, the neutralist groups in the Civil War, and many Whigs in the 1670s and 1680s. It was also the preference of republicans such as John Milton, who admired the Dutch republic and longed to see the same oligarchic civic humanism develop in England. Most dramatically, it was the ideal of democratic groups such as the Levellers, who wanted to make governors more accountable and government subservient to the liberties of a sovereign people, and who therefore urged devolution of power to elected local magistrates and juries. But these 'Country' ideologies were incompatible with the development of a global empire. The expansion into the West Indies and along the eastern seaboard of North America (from Carolina to the St Lawrence); into extensive trade networks with South America, West Africa, India, and Indonesia; even the protection of the vital trades with the southern and eastern Mediterranean all required strong naval and military power. This could only be sustained by a massive increase in the ability of the State to tax and to wage war. It was the combined threat of Louis XIV and the exiled James II after 1689 to introduce popery and arbitrary government which finally forced through the necessary constitutional and political changes. The Stuart century was one of unresolved tensions.

Chapter 7
Intellectual and Religious Life

For the Church of England, if not for the monarchy, the seventeenth century was an age of disillusionment. By the time of the Glorious Revolution of 1688 it had lost the intellectual, moral, and spiritual authority it had acquired by 1603. Intellectually, Anglicanism was on the offensive at the beginning of the century. The generation living through the events of 1559, ending England's becoming officially Protestant, witnessed a settlement cobbled together to meet political necessities, a hybrid of Protestant doctrine and Catholic practice. The criticisms of the first generation of Puritans were the more telling because their Marian exile allowed them to speak from experience of the purity of the Continental reformed Churches. The new generation of the 1590s and 1600s had known no other Church, and had come to love the rhythms of the Anglican liturgical year and the cadences of Cranmer's liturgy. The work of John Jewel, Richard Hooker, and Lancelot Andrewes presented the Church of England as the best of all Churches, claiming an apostolic descent and an uninterrupted history from the Celtic Church which gave it a greater authority than that of the schismatic Protestant Churches, and a superiority over Rome in that it had sloughed off the corruptions and failings of the Roman Catholic Church just as it had sloughed off the usurped authority of the bishops of Rome. The Church of England had an authority as ancient and as apostolic as Rome's, and a practice more true to the injunctions of Christ. These were claims which the Puritans did not find easy to meet.

The Acquiescence of Dissent

Puritans displayed an increasing willingness to work within the Church. Their response to James I's accession, the Millenary Petition, called only for modifications within the existing framework. At the Hampton Court Conference of 1604, in which James presided over a meeting of bishops and Puritans, discussion was entirely about how to make the episcopal national Church more effectively evangelical. Puritans yearned for a godly prince who, like the Emperor Constantine 1,200 years before, would bring good order to his State, and promote and protect true religion. They chafed for more to do, rather than for less. They worked within the Church and not against it. Even the 5 per cent of the nation who made up the Catholic recusants succumbed to an intellectual onslaught led by Anglican divines. The greatest single debate on any issue in the first quarter of the century was over the duties of Catholics to take the oath of allegiance and to eschew papal claims to command their political allegiance. Anglican arguments prevailed and the Catholics, while holding to their faith, abandoned political resistance. The Gunpowder Plot was the last real popish plot. As English Catholicism became controlled less by militant clergy and more by a prudent peerage and gentry, its pacifism and political acquiescence grew.

Protestant unity, if not uniformity, was retained until the Long Parliament. Puritans added their own practices to those of the Church, but the number who opted out and set up conventicles or assemblies in defiance of the Church was extremely small. Some hundreds, perhaps thousands, moved to New England rather than submit to the narrow interpretation of Anglican practice required by Archbishop Laud. But there was no schism.

The Civil War and interregnum years saw the disintegration not only of Anglicanism, but of English Puritanism. The structure of the Church of England was abolished (bishops, church courts) or proscribed (the

Prayer Book, the celebration of Christmas or Easter). Cathedrals were turned into preaching centres or secularized (used as barracks, prisons, or shopping arcades). In thousands of parishes the old services and celebrations were carried on despite the proscriptions. But the Church leaders lost their nerve. The bishops fled, hid, or remained silent. They were not replaced as they died. By 1660 the survivors were all over 70 years of age, and Church of England bishops were an endangered species.

But those who dreamed of replacing Anglicanism with a Calvinist Church like those of Massachusetts, Scotland, or Geneva were disappointed. The Presbyterian system conceived by Parliament was stillborn. The chaos of the Civil War created a bewildering variety of sects and gathered churches. The Baptists, one of the few strong underground Churches before 1640, spread widely via the army. Many new groups denied Calvinist notions of an Elect predestined to salvation, and proclaimed God's Grace to be freely available. Some even proclaimed universal salvation. Such groups were most evident in London and other, provincial cities. The largest of all the sects was that of the Quakers, whose informal missionary evangelism in the countryside gained thousands of adherents in the 1650s: denouncing the formalization of religion, and the specious authority of 'hireling priests' in their 'steeple houses', the Quakers urged people to find the divine spark within themselves, the Holy Spirit which came direct to the Christian, mediated neither by the Church nor by Scripture. Their hatred of formal worship and of tithes led them into widespread campaigns of militant passive disobedience. One of their leaders, James Nayler, was tried for blasphemy by the second Protectorate Parliament in 1656. Although he escaped the sentence of death, he was subject to a variety of severe physical punishments, Parliament taking several hours to contemplate which bits of him should be sliced or cut off.

Anglican Disillusionment

There was no recovering the old triumphalism after 1660. The Church might be outwardly restored to its ancient forms at the Restoration, but it had neither the self-assurance nor the power to reimpose a general uniformity. Anglican apologetics was defensive and edgy. With the disappearance of High Commission and the rust of disuse settled in its diocesan courts, the Church lacked the weapons to punish defaulters. The ignominy of its abolition left it institutionally enfeebled. In 1660 the celebration of Easter and the ubiquitous return of maypoles may have been spontaneous and have shown signs of their deep roots in popular culture. But those who chose to defy the Church were not going to be forced back into its assemblies. The decision in 1662 not to broaden its appeal by adapting its liturgy and by softening episcopal pretensions drove two thousand clergy out of the Church. Despite the attempts to prevent unlawful conventicles, the Baptists, Quakers, and other radicals were not to be uprooted. Even more important, the tens of thousands of 'Dissenters' of 1662 who were within the moderate Puritan tradition re-examined whether their desire to be part of a national Church (though not the one on offer) outweighed their desire for a pure worship of God. In the 1580s and the 1600s they had preferred to 'tarry for the magistrate', to stay in the Church, and to wait for better times. In Restoration England, they came more and more to opt for separation. In the early seventeenth century they found 'much piety in Babylon'; now they abandoned such temporizing and went into schism. The Toleration Act of 1689 was the formal recognition of the fact of religious pluralism. Unable to punish those who were not its members, and unable to compel men and women to be its members, the Church of England was a spent spiritual force.

In the early and mid-seventeenth century, most intellectuals and most governors believed that there was a divine imperative to bring godliness, good discipline, and order to the English nation. God was guiding His people towards a Promised Land of peace and justice in which they would love and worship Him as it was their duty to do. The vision of a better world that could be built by human response to the divine challenge was shared by James and Charles I, by Wentworth and Laud, by Pym and Cromwell. All political writings were suffused by the immanence of God in his Creation, by a deep sense of God's activity in human history and in his providences, his signs of himself. Shakespeare's plays, Donne's poems, the thoughts of Henry Parker and the young John Milton all proclaim the same point: the plays of Marlowe are the exceptions that prove the rule.

No such hopes survived the interregnum. The trauma of regicide left few royalists with faith in the providence of God; the much deeper sense of betrayal experienced by the radicals in 1660 largely explains their political quiescence thereafter. Psychologically, the pain of betrayal after such visible testimonies of divine favour was too great. Instead, most of the Puritans and their heirs internalized the kingdom of God. They accepted the world as the domain of sin and of imperfectibility. Within this vale of tears, each person must seek personal peace by building a temple of grace within himself or herself. This acceptance of the limits of what Church and State could achieve dominated the ideology of the late seventeenth century. It is apparent in the way Charles II's jaundiced view of the world was combined with his deep personal mysticism, in the latitudinarianism of the bishops and of the clerical establishment, and in the Dissenters' abandonment of the quest for a national Church. A few men continued to seek the millennium (Sir Isaac Newton combined his successful search for physical laws with an unsuccessful search for the dating of the Second Coming from the runes in the Book of Revelation), but most settled for making the most of things as they were. John Milton heroically confronted a God who appeared to have guided his people in the 1640s and 1650s only to betray them in 1660. *Paradise Lost* looked at the Omnipotent Creator who let man fall; *Paradise Regained* looked at the temptation of Christ in the wilderness, at the false worldly ways in which Man might proclaim the gospel. Perhaps republicans had been tempted into the wrong paths. *Samson Agonistes*, most poignantly of all, studied a man given great gifts by God who failed to use them in His service. Just as Samson dallied with Delilah and was shorn of his strength, so the republicans had been distracted by the things of the flesh in the 1650s and had missed their chance to do God's will. But the more typical Puritan work of the Restoration is Bunyan's *Pilgrim's Progress*, which concerns the individual's personal search for peace and salvation.

Christianity Depoliticized

Christianity was being depoliticized and demystified. The characteristic Anglican tracts of the late seventeenth century had titles like *The Reasonableness of Christianity* and *Christianity Not Mysterious*. Where God had been in the very warp and woof of nature and life, He now became the creator who set things going, and the spirit who worked within individuals and kept them obedient to moral rules. Sermons stressed the merits of neighbourliness and charity. Ministers were encouraged to preach that religious duties meant being kind to old people and animals rather than preaching about the transformation of the world. From the Dissenting side, John Locke, pleading for religious toleration, defined a church as a voluntary society of men, meeting together to worship God in such fashion as they deemed appropriate. Religion had become an unthreatening matter, almost a hobby. The authorities need not concern themselves with what consenting adults did in private meetings. The Puritans of previous generations could not have conceived anything so anaemic.

This dilution of religious energies, this breakdown of a world-view dominated by religious imperatives, can be seen in literature and in science. Restoration theatre differs from Jacobean not in its vulgarity or even in its triviality so much as in its secularism. Metaphysical poetry, which rooted religious experience in the natural world, gave way to a religious poetry either more cerebral and coolly rational, or else more ethereal and other-worldly.

Stuart Britain

10. St Paul's Cathedral under construction (c.1690). Wren's masterpiece replaced the old cathedral destroyed in the Great Fire

The Visual Arts

Secularization was also an aspect of change in the visual arts. Tudor and Stuart country houses emphasized paternalistic Christian values, being built around a great hall in which the household and a wider community gathered to do business and to eat together. There might be a 'high table', reflecting hierarchy and degree, but there was an easy informality of social relations. By the late seventeenth century, new houses had 'withdrawing' rooms and private dining rooms, while servants and other members of the household were given separate quarters. Houses were set in spacious parks surrounded by high walls and patrolled by gamekeepers. Royal palaces showed the way in these developments.

The seventeenth century, like the sixteenth, saw little church building. Perhaps a majority of all new churches were those needed in London after the Great Fire of 1666. There was, however, a stark contrast between the intensity and devotional emphasis of early Stuart churches and chapels such as the one at Peterhouse, Cambridge, and the coolness, light, and rationalist air of Sir Christopher Wren's London churches. Allegorical stained glass and dark wood panelling gave way to marble. The recumbent effigies of souls at rest gave way to an upright statuary of men and women reflecting on their moral duties.

In all the visual arts, the influence of the Counter-Reformation art of Spain, Spanish Italy, and the Spanish Netherlands – an ornateness that bound together the natural and the supernatural worlds – gave way to the influences of Louis XIV's France: self-indulgent, revelling in its own material extravagance. In the early seventeenth century, artists, musicians, and poets joined forces to produce the masque, an entertainment that sought to bring together the world of classical civilization and Christian values, of audiences drawn into the action as performers, a merging of fantasy and reality. The power of the illusion was so great in the case of Inigo Jones and Ben Jonson's masques for

Charles I that the king came to believe that his own piety and virtue would soon infect his subjects, and that order and uniformity could be as easily achieved in the State as on the stage. No such illusion bedevilled the artifice of the opera, the equivalent art form of the late seventeenth century. While early Stuart writers wrestled with the heroic and the tragic, late Stuart writers turned to the domesticated homiletics of the novel and to the mock epics of Dryden and later of Pope.

Science

Restoration science was just as secularized. In the 1640s and 1650s, scientists had sought what they termed 'a great instauration'. Drawing on the ideas of Francis Bacon, and led by visionary social engineers such as Samuel Hartlib and the Bohemian exile Comenius, the scientific establishment was lionized by the Puritan politicians and undertook to build a Brave New World. Man would tame and gain dominion over the natural world. Medical advances would vanquish disease, agricultural advances would conquer hunger and want. The reformation of justice and of education would bring man into peaceful enjoyment of the new order. It was yet another facet of Protestant eschatology, and the scientific Zion, like other Zions, evaporated in 1660. The later seventeenth century in the Royal Society was an age not of visions but of piecemeal enquiry and improvement. Francis Bacon's principles of exact observation, measurement, and of inductive reasoning, refined by the Frenchman René Descartes, allowed major advances in the classification and study of plant and animal life. William Harvey's discovery of the circulation of the blood, just before the Civil War, led on to a series of advances in the knowledge of anatomy and physiology in the second half of the century. Isaac Newton's *Philosophiae Naturalis Principia Mathematica* (1687) was the basis of understanding of the physical laws for two hundred years, and the work of Robert Boyle in chemistry and Robert Hooke in geology created new disciplines on the basis of extensive experimentation and measurement. The advance of the physical sciences hit hard at the older mysteries. The discovery of the geometrical movement of heavenly bodies destroyed the credibility of astrology in intellectual circles. It is astonishing how quickly the discovery of natural laws bred a confidence that *everything* had a natural explanation. The realm of magic, of witches and spells, was abandoned by the educated. Within a generation of 1640 the prosecution of witches almost ceased. This was not because the people at large ceased to believe in curses and in magic, but because it was impossible to secure convictions from sceptical judges and jurors. Science and technology did not in fact advance on all fronts. The economy remained almost wholly dependent on human and animal muscle-power. No progress was made towards harnessing steam, let alone gas or electricity, as energy sources. The extraction of minerals from the ground and the smelting of ore contributed another technological bottle-neck. Science was changing attitudes, not transforming the economy.

Political Thought

Political thought was being secularized too. Thomas Hobbes stripped sovereignty of its moral basis; in *Leviathan* (1651), the concept of legitimacy as the justification of political authority was replaced by a concentration on *de facto* power and the ability to afford protection to the subjects who lived under this power. Machiavelli remained an odious name but his ideas became more and more persuasive as a counter to the divine-right pieties of Robert Filmer and of Stuart apologists.

The English Revolution does, then, stand as a turning-point. It may have achieved little that any of the parties sought after or fought for. It may have done even less to transform political and social institutions. But it deeply affected the intellectual values, at least of the political elite. An age which derived its momentum from Christian humanism, from chivalry, from a reverential antiquarianism, gave way to an age of pragmatism and individualism. When John Locke wrote in his second *Treatise of Government* (1690) that 'all men are naturally in a state of perfect freedom to order their actions and dispose of their possessions and persons as they think fit without asking the leave or depending upon the will of any man', he was proclaiming a message only made possible by the disillusionment with old ideals, but a message which was to make much possible in the decades to come.

Further Reading

Political and Constitutional History

G. E. Aylmer, *The Levellers in the English Revolution* (London, 1975), a brief essay and key texts.

B. Coward, *The Stuart Age* (London, 1980), the best introductory survey.

G. Donaldson, *Scotland: James V to James VII* (Edinburgh, 1965).

C. H. Firth, *Oliver Cromwell and the Rule of the Puritans* (Oxford, 1900).

F. M. G. Higham, *Catholic and Reformed: A Study of the Church of England 1559–1662* (London, 1962), an excellent study of religious thought.

C. Hill, *The World Turned Upside Down* (Harmondsworth, 1973), re-creates the world of the religious radicals of the 1650s.

D. Hirst, *Authority and Conflict 1603–58* (London, 1985).

S. J. Houston, *James I* (London, 1973).

J. R. Jones, *The Revolution of 1688 in England* (London, 1972).

J. R. Jones, *Country and Court 1658–1714* (London, 1979).

J. P. Kenyon, *The Stuarts* (London, 1958).

J. P. Kenyon, *The Popish Plot* (London, 1972).

M. MacCurtain, *Tudor and Stuart Ireland* (Dublin, 1972), a short analysis.

J. Miller, *James II: A Study in Kingship* (London, 1978).

T. W. Moody, F. X. Martin, and F. J. Byrne (eds), *A New History of Ireland, vol. iii 1534–1691* (Oxford, 1976), a long narrative.

J. S. Morrill, *The Revolt of the Provinces* (London, 1976).

R. Ollard, *The Image of the King: Charles I and Charles II* (London, 1979).

C. Russell, *The Crisis of Parliaments 1509–1660* (Oxford, 1971).

A. Woolrych, *Battles of the English Civil War* (London, 1961).

A. B. Worden (ed.), *Stuart England* (London, 1986).

Social, Economic, and Cultural

J. Bossy, *The English Catholic Community 1570–1850* (London, 1975).

C. Clay, *Economic Expansion and Social Change: England 1500–1700* (Cambridge, 1984).

D. C. Coleman, *The Economy of England 1450–1750* (Oxford, 1977), a brilliantly crisp synthesis.

C. Hill, *Society and Puritanism in Pre-Revolutionary England* (London, 1964).

J. Hook, *The Baroque Age* (London, 1976).

P. Laslett, *The World We Have Lost* (London, 1971).

T. C. Smout, *A History of the Scottish People 1560–1830* (London, 1969).

M. Spufford, *Small Books and Pleasant Historie: Popular Fiction and its Readers in 17th Century England* (London, 1981).

L. Stone, *The Crisis of the Aristocracy* (abridged version, Oxford, 1967).

R. Strong, *Van Dyck: Charles I on Horseback* (London, 1972).

K. V. Thomas, *Religion and the Decline of Magic* (London, 1971).

C. Webster, *The Great Instauration* (London, 1970).

K. Wrightson, *English Society 1580–1680* (London, 1982), recreates the mental world of the seventeenth-century villager.

Documents and Contemporary Texts

J. Aubrey, *Brief Lives*, many editions but e.g. (Harmondsworth, 1962).

J. Evelyn, *Diary*, various editions and extracts, principally the edition by E. S. de Beer, 6 vols (Oxford, 1955).

R. Gough, *The History of Myddle* (Harmondsworth, 1981), a splendid evocation of life in a seventeenth-century parish, written by a local farmer.

J. P. Kenyon, *The Stuart Constitution* (Cambridge, 1962), for texts and stimulating commentary.

S. Pepys, *Diary*, various editions, but all previous ones superseded by that of R. C. Latham and W. Matthews, 11 vols (London, 1970–83).

The Illustrated Pepys, ed. R. C. Latham (London, 1978), a marvellous sampler.

J. Thirsk and J. P. Cooper, *Seventeenth-Century Economic Documents* (Oxford, 1972).

Bibliography

M. F. Keeler, *Bibliography of British History: Stuart Period, 1603–1714* (Oxford, 1970), a comprehensive guide to publications up to 1960.

J. S. Morrill, *Critical Bibliographies in Modern History: Seventeenth Century Britain* (Folkestone, 1980), complements Keeler and offers comments on the works discussed.

Stuart Britain

Chronology

1625	Death of James I; accession of Charles I and marriage to Henrietta Maria, sister of Louis XIII of France
1626–9	War with France
1628	Petition of Right; publication of Harvey's work on the circulation of the blood; assassination of Buckingham
1629	Charles I dissolves Parliament, determines to govern without one
1630	Large-scale emigration to Massachusetts begins
1633	William Laud translated to be archbishop of Canterbury
1634–40	Ship Money case
1637	Hampden's case supports Charles I's claim to collect Ship Money
1637–40	Breakdown of Charles's government of Scotland and two attempts to impose his will by force
1640	Long Parliament summoned
1641	Remodelling of government in England and Scotland; abolition of conciliar courts, abolition of prerogative taxation, triennial bill, Grand Remonstrance; rebellion of Ulster Catholics
1642	King's attempt on the Five Members; his withdrawal from London; the 19 Propositions; the resort of arms: Civil War
1643	King's armies prosper; Scots invade on side of Parliament
1644	Parliamentary armies prosper, especially in the decisive battle of the war, Marston Moor (June)
1645	'Clubmen' risings of armed neutrals threaten both sides; Royalist armies disintegrate, but parliamentary forces reorganized (New Model Army)
1646	King surrenders to the Scots; bishops and Book of Common Prayer abolished, Presbyterian Church established
1647	Army revolt; radical movements criticize parliamentary tyranny; king prevaricates
1648	Second Civil War: Scots now side with the king and are defeated; provincial risings (Kent, Colchester, South Wales, Yorks., etc.) crushed
1649	Trial and execution of Charles I: England a republic

1649–53	Government by sovereign single-chamber assembly; the Rump Parliament thoroughly purged of royalists and moderates
1649–50	Oliver Cromwell conquers Ireland (Drogheda massacre)
1650–2	Oliver Cromwell conquers Scotland (battles of Dunbar and Worcester)
1651	Thomas Hobbes's *Leviathan* published
1652–4	First Dutch War
1653	Oliver Cromwell dissolves Rump, creates the Nominated or Barebones Parliament; it surrenders power back to him, and he becomes Lord Protector under a paper constitution (*Instrument of Government*)
1655–60	War with Spain
1655	Royalist insurrection (Penruddock's rising) is a complete failure
1657	*Instrument of Government* replaced by a parliamentary paper constitution, the *Humble Petition and Advice*; Oliver Cromwell rejects title of king and remains lord protector, but nominates his own House of Lords
1658	Oliver Cromwell dies and is succeeded by his son Richard
1659	Richard Cromwell overthrown by the army; Rump restored but displeases many in the army
1660	Charles II restored
1662	Church of England restored; Royal Society receives its Charter
1663	Failure of first royal attempt to grant religious toleration
1665–7	Second Dutch War
1665	Great Plague (final major outbreak)
1666	Great Fire of London
1667	Milton's *Paradise Lost* published
1672–3	Failure of second royal attempt to grant religious toleration
1672–4	Third Dutch War
1674	Grain bounties introduced (England self-sufficient in food)
1678	Titus Oates and the Popish Plot; part 1 of Bunyan's *Pilgrim's Progress* published

1678–81	The Exclusion crisis; emergence of Whig and Tory parties
1683	The Rye House Plot; Whigs proscribed
1685	Charles II dies; accession of James II; rebellion by Charles II's Protestant bastard, the duke of Monmouth, fails
1687	James II's Declaration of Indulgence; Tories proscribed; Newton's *Principia Mathematica* published
1688	James II's son born; William of Orange invades: James takes flight; accession of William III (of Orange) and Mary

Index

Page numbers in *italics* refer to illustrations or captions. There may also be textual references on the same page.

Visit the
VERY SHORT
INTRODUCTIONS
Web site

www.oup.co.uk/vsi

➤ **Information** about all published titles

➤ News of **forthcoming books**

➤ **Extracts** from the books, including titles
not yet published

➤ **Reviews** and views

➤ **Links** to other **web sites** and main
OUP web page

➤ Information about **VSIs in translation**

➤ **Contact** the editors

➤ **Order** other **VSIs** on-line